Keeping and Breeding ZEBRA FINCHES

THE·COMPLETE·TYPE·STANDARD·GUIDE

Keeping and Breeding ZEBRA FINCHES

THE·COMPLETE·TYPE·STANDARD·GUIDE

Chris Blackwell

BLANDFORD PRESS

LONDON · NEW YORK · SYDNEY

First published in the UK 1988 by Blandford Press
Artillery House, Artillery Row, London SW1P 1RT

Copyright © 1988 Chris Blackwell

Distributed in the United States by
Sterling Publishing Co, Inc,
2 Park Avenue, New York, NY 10016

Distributed in Australia by
Capricorn Link (Australia) Pty Ltd
PO Box 665, Lane Cove, NSW 2066

British Library Cataloguing in Publication Data

Blackwell, Chris, *1951*
    Keeping and breeding zebra finches : the
    complete type standard guide.
    1. Zebra finch
    I. Title
    636.6′862   SF473.Z42

ISBN 0 7137 1959 1

Designed by Kathryn S.A. Booth   ·
Typeset by Inforum Ltd., Portsmouth
Printed and bound in Great Britain by Biddles Ltd.,
Guildford and Kings Lynn.

Contents

Acknowledgements

Among the birds used to illustrate this book are specimens bred by K. Bamford; Mr and Mrs B.C.E. Binns; R.W. and C. Blackwell; T.E. Broderick; B. Debling; P. Dumville; A. Dunford; L. Harper; K. and M. Lockwood; D. and G. Massey; W. Parke; E. Payne; A.A. Smith and J. Woodcock.

All photographs are copyright C.B. Studios. The map on p. 8 is taken from *Field Guide to the Birds of Australia*, Graham Pizzey, published by Collins; the map on p. 9 is taken from *The World*, Dudley Stamp, © Geographical Publications Ltd; the drawings on pp. 134 and 135 are © Zebra Finch Society.

The author would also like to thank Mike Wrenn for his help and advice on matters relating to inheritance and the matings list, and P. Dumville; L. Harper; K. and M. Lockwood; D. and G. Massey and A.A. Smith, for allowing birds in their possession to be photographed specifically for inclusion in this book.

The Zebra Finch Society are also gratefully acknowledged for granting permission to reproduce parts of their standards and rules in this book.

Finally, thanks are due to all Zebra Finch breeders and exhibitors in general. Without their collective knowledge, encouragement and interest, it would have been impossible to compile this book.

Chris Blackwell 1987

Introduction

The Zebra Finch (*Poephila guttata*) is a species of small grass-finch about 4in (10cm) in length. It has a distinctive red beak, usually brighter in cocks, a black and white barred tail, white rump and black tear marks. The head, neck, back and wings are generally grey or greyish-brown, and the feet and legs orangey-red in both sexes. The throat and breast of cock birds is pale grey, detailed with fine lateral black lines extending across the full width of the throat and breast. These zebra stripes are terminated with a broader black band, known as the breast bar. Additionally cocks display quadrant-shaped, deep orange or chestnut-coloured, cheek patches on the face, and have chestnut-coloured flank markings, decorated with small white spots, extending from the wing butts to the rump. Underparts on cock birds, from the breast bar to the vent, are white or off-white, with hens having buff-coloured underparts and a grey throat and upper breast.

These birds originate from Australia where they are found occurring naturally in most areas apart from the extreme north, east and south-eastern coastal regions, and the south-western tip of the country. Their habitat tends to be scrub forest, grasslands and open country, but they will colonise any region which offers the required climatic and dietry needs. It would seem that in the wild Zebra Finches prefer regions with less than 40in (115cm) annual rainfall, despite some of these wetter areas providing quite abundant food supplies. Small seeds, such as those of grasses, form the basis of their diet, although they will eat small insects and fruit given the opportunity. Within ornithological circles, such a robust and common little bird often merits only a few lines in a handbook of Australian birds, but in avicultural circles Zebra Finches have become one of the most popular and widely bred birds in the world today.

A pair of Normal or Grey Zebra Finches. This is the appearance of Zebra Finches in their wild state

Distribution of Zebra Finches in the wild in Australia

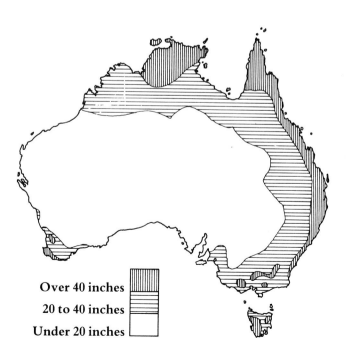

Over 40 inches
20 to 40 inches
Under 20 inches

Annual rainfall map for Australia

Zebra Finches are gregarious, preferring to live, feed and breed in flocks or colonies. Their breeding cycle is dependent on the food supply available, rather than being geared to the seasons. Rainfall is probably the most important single factor in creating adequate food supplies, and therefore Zebra Finches in the wild will commence breeding at any time of year, providing there has been sufficient rain. Their tolerance of a wide range of different conditions, and willingness to breed, make them particularly suitable avicultural subjects, even for quite inexperienced fanciers. However, by breeding them in controlled conditions, it is also possible to produce birds to a given standard for the purposes of competitive exhibition. This can make keeping and breeding these birds every bit as challenging as the management of rarer and more exotic species.

The vast majority of Zebra Finches available to birdkeepers have been bred and reared in captivity and are now regarded as a truly domesticated species. When large numbers of one species are bred in controlled conditions, it is usual for colour mutations to be produced occasionally. With careful management, these mutations can be selectively bred and become established colour forms. This is the case with Zebra Finches, where, in addition to the Grey or Normal form which is found in the wild, several other colours are now generally available to birdkeepers. This makes it quite possible to maintain an interesting and visually varied collection simply by keeping this one species of bird.

Anyone interested in keeping Zebra Finches should always remember that they are quite unique when compared to other birds commonly found in aviculture. This makes it important, when seeking advice on these birds, to be guided by people with sound practical experience of keeping Zebra Finches. Many fanciers from other sections of the hobby will readily offer advice and, although well meant, much of it is quite inappropriate. During the time I have been keeping, breeding and exhibiting these birds, they have never lost their basic charm and appeal. I am sure, given the right sort of guidance, anyone, who wishes to keep visually attractive birds which have character, will find Zebra Finches ideal subjects.

1 Stock Selection

Zebra Finches can usually be purchased from a number of different sources as most good pet shops and bird farms, in addition to private breeders, will offer Zebras for sale. Exactly which source will be the most suitable depends largely on the requirements of the buyer. For example, it is not usually possible to buy exhibition-type stock from a pet shop, and for this purpose private breeders and exhibitors should be approached.

Before making any purchase it is wise to inspect the stock personally. Zebra Finches should be bright-eyed, full of life and active at all times. Birds which sit huddled together and seem sleepy or lethargic are usually unwell and may only live for a few days. The majority of colours generally available are quite suitable for anyone wanting to establish a mixed collection, and most should be bought as pairs of the same colour. The general exception to this is in the case of Dominant Dilutes, where it is usual to mate a Dominant Silver to a Normal and a Dominant Cream to a Fawn. Often, when two different colour mutations are mated together, the resulting young will all be Normal Greys. This can prove to be quite a disappointment if it is your intention to breed a wide range of different colours.

Sexing
In order to purchase pairs of birds, one must be able to differentiate between cocks and hens. This is quite easily done with most colours of Zebra Finches, as cock birds have distinctive markings in the form of orange or chestnut cheek patches, definite breast barring and chestnut side flanks. All these characteristic markings are absent on hens who only show tear marks and tail barrings. In the case of White Zebra Finches, where there are no characteristic markings, birds may

be sexed visually by their beaks which are a shade brighter on most cocks. Some Pieds can be a little difficult to sex if they carry a lot of white markings, as these could mask the face, breast and flank areas of the birds so that no characteristic markings would be visible. Penguin Zebras do not show breast barring on the cocks, but, of course, they still retain the cheek patches and side flanks. Many Dilutes have much paler characteristic markings, but these should still be quite evident on close inspection. In addition to the marking differences, Zebra Finches can be sexed by the display ritual of the cock birds. This consists of uttering a rapid, if tuneless, succession of 'notes' and adopting a more dominant posture than usual.

Ringed Birds

Birds offered for sale will often be wearing a closed metal ring. These rings can only be fitted to young birds in the nest and most will indicate the year during which the bird was bred and also the person who bred the bird. The colour of the ring is the important factor in determining the age of the bird. In Britain, rings specifically for Zebra Finches can be obtained through the Zebra Finch Society and these change colour on a nine-year cycle, as follows: yellow, turquoise, red, gold, pink, dark blue, orange, green and violet; commencing with yellow in 1986, which will then be repeated in 1995. Inscribed on each ring is the code number of the breeder of the bird, a number for identifying each individual bird and the letters Z and S, inserted in between which is another number. This number is a further check on the age of the bird, as it is the last digit of the year during which the bird was bred, e.g. a bird bred in 1984 and rung with a Z.F.S. ring will have a green closed ring bearing the figures Z4S, whereas a bird bred in 1993 will have a green ring inscribed with Z3S. It is prudent not to buy birds which are more than two years old, as Zebra Finches have a limited life span and, on average, will only live for three or four years.

Purchasing Birds

Zebra Finches can be purchased at any time of year, although mid-summer usually affords the buyer the largest selection of stock. When specific colours or exhibition stock are required, it may be necessary to contact breeders specialising in Zebra

Finches. Contacts can often be made through Zebra Finch specialist societies or local cage-bird clubs, but remember that successful exhibitors may have many outstanding orders for birds and often cannot supply everyone immediately. For anyone hoping to establish an exhibition stud, it is advisable to seek advice from a more experienced local Zebra Finch fancier if at all possible.

When first starting in the hobby, fanciers will simply require a pair, or a few pairs of birds of a particular colour. Should one become more interested in the exhibition side of the fancy, the requirement will be for birds which display particular features that will improve or complement existing stock. Such birds tend to be in great demand and breeders often need to be patient when trying to build up an exhibition stud. It should be remembered that it is not always champion breeders who have the best birds for sale; many novices breed good quality stock and they are much less likely to have long waiting lists of buyers.

Before deciding to buy exhibition-quality birds, it is wise to gain some experience of Zebra Finches by obtaining a few breeding pairs of non-pedigree stock. Once a little practical experience has been acquired, the quality of the stock can be upgraded. If you already own birds which have bred well, these are often best retained for possible use as foster parents, as better quality stock can be more temperamental and newly acquired birds may take some time to adjust to your routine.

Before purchasing quality birds, try making a few enquiries; it may be possible to arrange a meeting with one or more established fanciers at forthcoming shows. This will not only permit birds to be viewed and compared, but also allow new acquaintances to be made. Never expect to buy the best birds owned by breeders; they may have spent years building up their strain and are unlikely to part with their winners. Additionally, those people who continually pester breeders to part with stock they wish to keep, rapidly become unpopular and tend to be avoided. The birds to look for are those closely related to winners, and most birdkeepers are only too happy to relate the 'life story' of their birds.

Prices charged for birds often vary considerably from fancier to fancier and birds cannot be assessed by their price tag. Every buyer has the right to refuse birds if they are unsuitable, but it is foolish to turn down cheap birds without actually seeing them first; they may well be a bargain. It is quite possible to establish a good stud of Zebra Finches without spending a lot of money provided you give the stock the chance to prove themselves. All too often breeders look at the first youngsters produced, decide they are not up to standard, dispose of the stock and look for fresh birds. Every pair bought should be given a fair chance and this means allowing their youngsters to breed before making any rash decisions. Often the best birds are produced among the second-generation youngsters, when the first-generation youngsters are mated to good quality unrelated birds. Generally speaking, beginners buy too many birds from too many different sources when first starting out.

Newly acquired birds, purchased from whatever source, must initially be housed separately from other stock. They should be treated with an antimite spray, or dusted with mite powder, to the specific instructions given by the manufacturer, as soon as possible after purchase, and the treatment repeated a week later. If, after a fortnight, the birds appear fit and healthy, they can be housed with other birds you may have, with very little chance of them passing on infectious diseases.

2 Accommodation and Housing

Before buying any birds it is essential to have suitable quarters in which to house them. Whether you plan to keep a single pair in the home, or have elaborate plans for a birdroom and garden aviary, accommodation must be made ready before any birds are acquired. This may seem to be an obvious statement, but it is surprising just how many people buy birds on impulse and then wonder where to keep them. Cages and flights which are hurriedly constructed, without careful forethought and planning, seldom cater ideally for the birds they are meant to house.

Cages

The best style of cage in which to house Zebra Finches is that of a box-type design. These have a solid top, back, sides and bottom, with just the front being of wire. Cages of this type protect the birds from excessive draughts and help them to feel more secure. A single stock cage should measure about 24in (60cm) in length, 15in (38cm) in height and 15in (38cm) in depth, this being large enough to house up to half a dozen individual birds, or one breeding pair. Individual box cages can be bought readymade, or, with a few basic carpentry skills and some simple tools, made exactly to your own specifications.

The wire fronts for these cages can be bought separately, and those advertised as Budgie fronts, which have a large, hinged door, and no headholes for hoppers, etc., tend to be the most suitable. A large door is invaluable during the breeding season, allowing for easy positioning and inspection of the nest box inside the cage, while the absence of headholes prevents the birds accidentally escaping. If you have the ability to use a soldering iron and solder, you may prefer to buy punch bar and tinned wire in order to make your own cage fronts. Punch bar, with holes drilled every ⅝in (16mm), and either 16-gauge or 14-gauge tinned wire, is ideal for most Zebra Finches. Cage fronts should be bought or made before starting to construct the cages themselves. It is easier to build a cage to meet the specifications of a wire front, than it is to alter a front to fit the cage. Usually cage fronts measuring 24in (60cm) in length and 12in (30cm) in height will be required.

The top, sides and bottom of cages are best constructed out of 9mm exterior-quality plywood or, if preferred, white melamine-covered plywood. The body of the cage should allow space not only for the cage front, but also for the inclusion of a top rail, bottom rail, removable tray below the bottom rail, and a gap of about ½in (12mm) between the top of the cage front and the bottom of the top rail. The sides of the cage therefore need to be the height of the cage front, measured from the top horizontal wire to the bottom horizontal wire, plus ½in, plus the height of the top rail (approximately ½in), plus the height of the bottom rail (approximately 1in or 25mm), plus the height of the removable tray, thus making the total height of the cage about 15in (38cm).

The top rail, bottom rail and front of the removable tray can be made from dressed softwood and should all be of equal thickness, about ½in (12mm), from front to back. When measuring the length of the top and bottom of the cage you must remember to add the thickness of both cage sides to the length of the wire front to find the total over-all length of the cage.

The back of the cage and the bottom of the removable tray need to be about 4mm thick, and plywood or laminated plywood are most usually used.

The order of construction is usually as follows: fix the sides of the cage to the bottom, using 1in panel pins, and then fix the top to the sides, to make a rectangle. After making sure the corners are at right-angles (90°), the back can be fixed, using ¾in panel pins. If desired, joints can be glued as well as pinned, to make the structure more robust. The top rail can then be fixed to the underside of the top, along the front edge of the cage, again using panel pins and glue. The bottom rail should be positioned to allow sufficient space for the removable tray to slide underneath, leaving a space equal to the height of the cage front plus ½in, between the bottom of the top rail and the top of the bottom rail. Once correctly positioned, the rail can be fixed by nailing 1in panel pins through the sides of the cage into the ends of the rail. All that then remains to be done is to make the removable tray, paint the interior of the cage, if laminated boards have not been used, and fix the wire front in position.

The method of fixing the front is to use the fixing wires which protrude above and below the front. There are usually eight of these, four at the top and four at the bottom. By drilling holes into the top and bottom rails in a position corresponding to the fixing wires, the front can be inserted. Firstly, push the top fixing wires fully up into the top rail, then position the bottom fixing wires directly above the holes in the bottom rail and press the front firmly down into position. Should the bottom fixing wires be a little too long, they can be trimmed so that the front can be fitted without bending. When drilling holes into the bottom rail, it is wise to drill right through the rail so that if sawdust or sand collects in the holes, it can be pushed out easily using a thin nail, allowing the front to fit properly. Failure to do this will either result in the fronts fitting badly, or you spending time and effort redrilling the fixing holes. If you are unable to buy cage fronts exactly to the length required, a slightly longer front can be trimmed to size by removing a few of the vertical wires from each end.

A typical breeding cage as used for Zebra Finches

The Birdroom

When constructing cages for a birdroom, it is usually beneficial to make them in blocks, which allows adjacent cages to be
separated by removable slides. This then offers the alternative
of having longer flight cages, or single breeding cages, as
required. If you do make blocks of cages, remember they will
need to be moved from time to time, so do not make them so
large that they cannot be manhandled easily. Blocks of cages
can be constructed in a similar manner to individual cages,
remembering to include runners between each cage for the
removable slides.

All cages must be fitted with at least two perches which, for

*Possible layout options for a birdroom: a) space for breeding cages; b) and c) space for
inside flight, breeding cages, show preparation cages or storage; d) space for seating or
storage; e) exterior door; f) interior wire safety door; g) windows; h) floor space; i)
and j) space necessarily wasted when cages are positioned on adjacent walls*

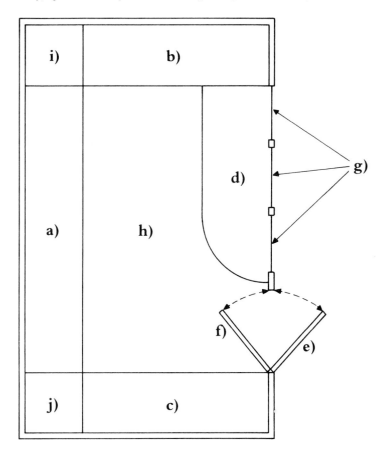

Zebra Finches, should be about ³/₈in (9mm) in diameter. Perches are usually positioned at each end of the cage, allowing sufficient clearance for the birds to sit normally on the perch without catching their tails on the end of the cage. It is important that food and water pots are not placed underneath perches, as they will become fouled by droppings. Natural twigs or round dowelling are most commonly used as perches and it is best to provide a variety of perch thicknesses so that birds can exercise their feet properly.

Square perches are quite popular with some fanciers and, if these cannot be bought 'off-the-shelf', they can easily be made by planing the sides off round ½in (12mm) dowelling. This does not need to be done very precisely, as imperfections and variations will be of benefit to the birds. The most common method of fixing perches is to brace them between the back of the cage and the inside of the wire cage front. Fixing may be assisted by tapping a headless panel pin into the end of the perch which is positioned against the back of the cage.

Other perches are available, which twist onto the wire cage front and are not supported by the back of the cage. These have proved quite popular with a number of birdkeepers, but, when used in conjunction with spot-welded cage fronts, the extra strain they place on the joints can lead to the vertical wires breaking loose. Perches may also be fastened to the back of the cage, using a screw, and left free at their front end, which helps prevent birds roosting up against the wire fronts. Whatever type of perch is used, they must always be securely fastened. Perches which continually fall down, because they do not fit properly, are useless and tend to make birds nervous.

Outdoor Aviaries

Outdoor aviaries and flights can be an attractive garden feature and countless hours of enjoyment may be had simply watching a mixed collection of Zebra Finches. It is important that outdoor aviaries are always sited on firm level ground, free from standing water, and the sections of the aviary must be securely fastened to the ground, to prevent damage in high winds. In order to be practical, aviaries will need to be at least 6ft (1.8m) in height, allowing easy entry for cleaning and maintenance. All wood used for outdoor structures must be treated with wood preservative, and retreated at least once a year. Birds should not be allowed to come into contact with freshly treated wood until the preservative has dried thoroughly. At least one side of the aviary should be solid, to afford some shelter from cold winds, and part of the roof must be covered to prevent seed and other foodstuffs becoming damp when it rains. If an aviary is built with a sloping roof, then corrugated plastic sheeting is ideal as a protective cover.

In most cases it is also necessary to build a frost-free shelter onto your aviary, and this may well mean providing some form of heating. Thermostatically controlled electric heaters are to be preferred as they are clean, easily controlled and unlikely to give off toxic fumes which are usually quite lethal to birds. Supplementary lighting, to extend the day length during the winter months, can be a great advantage and is fairly easy to fit once an electric supply has been installed.

Aviary sections are usually constructed on frameworks of $1\frac{1}{2} \times 1\frac{1}{2}$in (4 × 4cm) timber, and covered with $\frac{1}{2}$in (12mm) wire netting. In areas where cats or hawks are a nuisance, sections will need to be covered in wire netting on both sides and the two layers kept separated. The outside layer of netting may be of a slightly larger mesh to cut material costs. New wire netting is often quite bright and shiny, making it difficult to view the birds from outside the aviary. Visibility can be improved by painting the wire netting with non-toxic matt black paint, using an ordinary paint roller. Once all the aviary sections are completed, and the inside layer of netting is attached, they can be joined together, making sure there are no gaps through which the birds can escape. It is probably wisest to bolt the sections together so that the aviary can be dismantled and moved if necessary.

To secure the sections to the ground, they can be fastened onto large wooden beams, such as old railway sleepers, or onto a solid concrete base. Having erected the main body of the aviary, the outside layer of wire netting, if required, can be fastened in place. Aviary floors may be of natural earth, gravel or concrete, the latter two being slightly easier to manage, while natural earth offers birds an additional source of minerals and trace elements. If a solid concrete floor is not used, in order to prevent unwelcome visitors, in the form of mice and other rodents, $\frac{1}{2}$in wire netting will need to be fastened round the base of the aviary, along its whole perimeter, and set vertically downwards, to a depth of 12in (30cm) below ground level.

The edges of all wire netting fixed to the inside of aviaries and flights should be covered by thin strips of wood to prevent birds, especially those wearing rings on their legs, becoming caught and damaging themselves. Although it may seem unlikely that birds could become 'snared' on these small protrusions, it is quite common for birds to be injured in this manner.

It is always prudent to fit a safety porch around exterior aviary doors, to prevent birds escaping accidentally while you are entering or leaving the aviary.

Perches for aviaries can be more varied than those used in cages, ranging from about ¾in (18mm) in thickness to very thin slender twigs. Cover, in the form of bunches of heather, may also be provided in aviaries, together with small shrubs. However, too much greenery will often make viewing the birds very difficult.

While aviaries are very attractive, they do have their limitations. A flight measuring 6ft (1.8m) × 3ft (0.9m), and 6ft high, will accommodate about thirty or forty individual birds, but

Section of outdoor aviary, showing position of wire netting below ground level

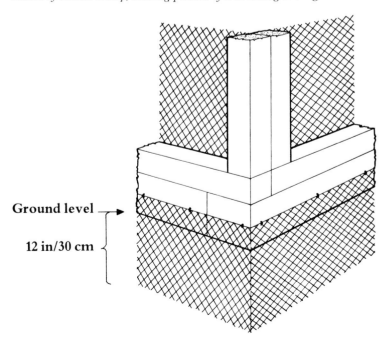

Ground level →

12 in/30 cm

only three or four breeding pairs. Additionally, there is no control over which birds mate with which, and therefore it is impossible to practise selective breeding or to keep accurate breeding records. Just because a cock helps a particular hen to rear her youngsters, it does not prove that he is their natural father; the hen may well have mated with another, more dominant, cock bird. A much more effective use of space, and greater control over matings, can be achieved by combining a birdroom and garden aviary. Indeed, many leading fanciers do not use outdoor aviaries at all for their birds, as selective breeding and exhibition preparation really require the birds to be housed in cages.

Any good quality garden shed can be converted into a birdroom, but, ideally, the best type of shed is one which has its door and windows all on the same side, rather than those which have windows along the front and a door at the end. Before installing cages in the chosen shed, it should be lined throughout, using good quality hardboard or plywood. Additional insulating material, such as polystyrene or glass fibre, can be placed between the shed wall and the lining, to prevent excessive heat loss during cold weather. It is important that the birdroom door shuts securely at both top and bottom. This is usually achieved by screwing two elongated wooden buttons onto the outside of the birdroom, one opposite the top of the door and one opposite the bottom. When rotated, these hold the door firmly closed.

During warm weather wooden doors tend to warp, allowing draughts, and also mice, to enter the birdroom when the weather turns colder again. Both mice and draughts can be harmful to birds, and should always be discouraged. However, all birdrooms must be adequately ventilated to prevent the atmosphere becoming musty. A number of simple ventilators are available commercially and one should be fitted into each end of the birdroom, but in such a position so that the birds will not be in a direct draught. During warm weather it may be necessary to open the birdroom door fully in order to prevent temperatures becoming excessively high. If the door is left open, it must be replaced by a wire door to keep out animals such as cats and dogs which may injure or frighten the birds. Ideally, birdrooms should not be allowed to reach temperatures above 27°C (80°F) although this is not always possible to prevent during very hot spells. Windows will need to be covered with a removable wire-netted frame on the inside, not only to prevent birds escaping if the windows are open or the glass is broken, but also to deny access to vermin or pests.

Heating and Lighting

It is a great advantage to have an electricity supply in a birdroom and this should be included in the design if possible. Obviously it is wise to have the basic installation carried out by a qualified electrician. The supply should be capable of running a lighting system, thermostatically controlled heating and provide two or more 13 amp sockets so that hospital cages and other appliances can be used in the birdroom. If possible, the birdroom should be kept to a minimum temperature of 5°C (40°F) at all times, and increased to 10°C (50°F) during the breeding season.

Another great advantage is to have a water supply laid on in a birdroom. In many cases this is not possible, but should the opportunity arise to plumb a sink into the birdroom, it is a very worthwhile addition.

Once the basic shed has been converted, cages can be installed. Exactly what cage layout is required depends largely on your own specific requirements, but a minimum of twelve breeding cages, and also space to house any young birds bred, should be included. Brick-built birdrooms can be just as effective as wooden structures, but are not as easily erected and generally more expensive.

It can seem quite an expensive business to build a birdroom, but it is always wise to construct the best you can afford. A well-made birdroom or aviary will last virtually a lifetime with only the minimum of maintenance, but a poor quality structure will require constant attention. Equally, well-made cages and aviaries will last for decades, provided they are properly maintained, but those 'cobbled' together as a last-minute afterthought will usually be scrapped after a couple of years. Birds are only at their best when housed in good conditions and cannot be enjoyed fully by their owners unless they are happy and contented in their surroundings.

3　Feeding

In order to survive, Zebra Finches require only a simple basic diet, but if you wish them to thrive, the provision of a good and varied diet is essential. While there are many additives and titbits available for birds, these are of little use unless a good basic diet is provided.

Seed

The first requirement is a good quality seed mixture, consisting of various millet seeds and small canary seed. Mixtures suitable for Zebra Finches and other small foreign seedeaters can be bought ready mixed from seed suppliers, or a mixture can be made up by buying the different seeds separately and mixing them exactly to the requirements of your birds. Possible millet seeds for a basic mixture include panicum or small yellow millet, pearl white millet, Japanese millet and Dakota millet. Of these, panicum millet is usually the most favoured seed, although tastes vary from birdroom to birdroom. As Zebra Finches tend to eat what they see other birds eating, a collection consisting just purely of Zebra Finches can be quite choosey about the food they eat. For a general basic seed I use the following mixture: 5 parts panicum millet, 1 part pearl white millet, 1 part Japanese millet and 2 parts small canary seed, with the proportion of panicum being increased when young birds start feeding themselves. I do not use Dakota millet, as many of my birds are reluctant to eat it, although other fanciers find their birds will eat it quite readily. Usually, when a mixture contains a seed which is disliked, Zebra Finches will knock it out of the seed pot, resulting in a lot of seed being scattered and wasted on the cage floor. Daily replenishment of seed pots is essential and, before topping up with fresh seed, any old husks from seed already eaten should be carefully blown out of the pot.

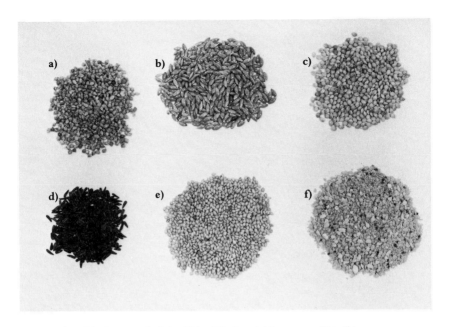

Some seeds and food commonly fed to Zebra Finches. (a) Japanese millet; (b) canary seed; (c) pearl white millet; (d) niger seed; (e) panicum or small yellow millet; (f) a typical proprietary brand of rearing food which only requires the addition of a little water before being given to the birds

The importance of using a consistently good quality seed supply cannot be overestimated. Fanciers who 'chop and change' from one seed supplier to another, in a search for cheap seed, often find their birds lack condition and vitality. Having found a reliable supplier of good quality seed, it is wise not to change without good reason. Being small birds, Zebra Finches eat very frequently and therefore must be given access to a source of seed at all times.

Other 'condition and tonic' seeds can also be provided if required. Niger seed is often used. This is a very oily seed, reputed to help in preventing hens from becoming egg bound. Birds may also appreciate a little foreign finch condition seed or wild seed mixture, but some will never even look at it. A great deal of investigation can be carried out into the nutritional properties of different seeds, but the most important factor is whether or not the birds will eat the seed provided. There is no point in supplying a seed which is heralded as giving the 'ideal balanced diet' unless the birds actually enjoy eating that type of seed. As long as the birds are fit and healthy, there is no problem with infertility, or dead in shell, and excessive amounts of seeds are not being wasted, then the seed mixture provided will probably be just as good as any of the alternatives available. One excellent method of testing the quality of seed is to try sprouting a small sample in a dish placed on a warm windowsill. Good seed should sprout easily and quickly within a few days of being moistened.

Water
The second essential of the diet is water. Although Zebra Finches can survive for relatively long periods without water, they must always have access to water when being kept in captivity. Ideally, fresh water should be given daily, either in open water pots, or in tubular drinkers. When open water pots are used, it is inevitable that the birds will bathe in the water, with the result that the water pot can be empty within a few hours of being replenished. Using tubular drinkers ensures that a constant supply of fresh water is available at all times, but, in addition to these, baths will need to be provided separately. Bathing is very important to Zebras; it helps keep feathers clean and in good condition and would also seem to be very enjoyable. Therefore, baths need to be made available at least once or twice every week and more often if possible. Tubular drinkers, apart from ensuring a constant supply of water, also allow water-soluble tonics to be added to the drinking water if required. There is little point in using a liquid vitamin preparation, or other conditioners, in the water if the birds are going bathe in it. One problem with giving tonics in the water for Zebra Finches is that because they can survive for long periods without drinking, if they dislike the taste of the additive, they will not drink until it has been replaced with untreated water. Naturally, when providing liquid tonics, all baths need to be removed as these offer an alternative water supply. Some fanciers are so particular about providing their birds with untreated water that they will collect rain water for their birds. Bearing in mind the current levels of pollution in the industrialized world, this is probably much more harmful than treated water from a normal drinking-water supply. If you are concerned about the quality of the mains water

supply, boiling it prior to use is probably the best remedy.

Grit

The third essential of the diet is grit and this is vitally important for all seedeating birds. Grit is used, in part, to grind the seed eaten by birds so that it can be digested. This grinding takes place in the gizzard, and therefore birds must have a plentiful supply of grit in order to digest their seed properly. Usually it is best to supply mineralised grit which also contains various trace elements that are equally essential for the well being of all living creatures. To this, limestone grit can also be added, which will add variety to the supply. It is not sufficient to supply grit and wait until it has all been eaten before providing any more. Grit pots should be replenished weekly, although there may seem to be plenty of grit still available. Birds show a marked preference for certain portions of the grit supplied and therefore grit which remains uneaten is probably unsuitable for their needs.

The grit supplied also provides the basic minerals for the production of eggshells and therefore breeding hens will require a plentiful supply of these minerals both before and during the breeding season. Cuttlefish bone, supplied both in solid and powdered form, is a useful additional supply of essential minerals. Most Zebra Finches will eat quite large quantities of cuttlefish bone and it should always be made available to them.

I also use crushed, domestic hens' eggshells for my birds prior and during the breeding season, but if these are to be used, it is imperative to process them properly. The eggshells should be washed as soon after being cracked as possible, then, when sufficient have been collected, they must be baked thoroughly in an oven, at a temperature of 150°C (300°F), for at least an hour. After cooling, they can be crushed into digestable-sized particles and added to the normal grit supplies. Failure to treat eggshells in the described manner may mean exposing your birds to micro-organisms which can be very harmful. One fancier I know experienced a serious setback when his young Zebras started suffering massive brain haemorrhaging at about three weeks of age. The cause of this was eventually traced back to organisms in the eggshells which he had been giving to his birds. These eggshells had only been dried, rather than baked, prior to use. On hearing this I stopped using crushed eggshells, but, after about three years, I became unhappy with the quality of the eggs being produced by a number of stock hens. The eggs seemed to have a rougher surface than usual, and although they contained a fertile embryo, the majority were very porous and consequently failed to hatch. This failing is usually due to a calcium deficiency, and since then I have used crushed, domestic hens' eggshells (which I wash and bake very thoroughly before use) in order to supply an additional source of this essential element. Simply by the addition of eggshells to the diet, the problem of stock hens producing badly shelled eggs has been completely cured, and there has been no sign of any unusual health problems in the birds.

Many fanciers are now advocating the use of various water-soluble calcium preparations to serve the same purpose. In theory these are fine, but to my mind they are very concentrated preparations and it is easy to overdose birds. Too much calcium is as harmful as too little and, where possible, I like to use natural sources to provide vitamins and minerals, as I believe this offers much less chance of overdosing the birds. A friend of mine used a soluble calcium preparation for his birds prior to one particular breeding season and had about 90 per cent dead in shell. This he blamed on the provision of extra calcium which was the only alteration he had made to his feeding and general management. Alternatively, I have known fanciers who, when faced with a large number of hens laying soft-shelled eggs, have cured the problem immediately by using a soluble calcium preparation.

Another useful source of minerals and trace elements is a piece of turf, placed earth side up in aviaries and flight cages, which most birds will greatly enjoy investigating. Charcoal is also widely used by many fanciers, myself included, and is reputed to 'sweeten' the digestive system, a pinch may be added to the grit pots about once a week. Among the other products which may be of assistance in providing additional trace elements and minerals for birds, are iodine blocks or nibbles, and pieces of cattle salt-licks.

Rearing Food
To get the best possible breeding results from Zebra Finches it

is necessary to provide some form of rearing food. There are many different types of rearing food available and countless more 'homemade' preparations which can be used successfully. I believe it is best to keep rearing foods simple, especially when first starting to keep birds. There is a tendency for birdkeepers to add a little bit of this and a little bit of that as time goes on, until the preparation of rearing foods has become extremely complicated. In all probability, many of the additives are serving no useful.purpose, but because their inclusion in the diet coincided with a particularly good breeding season, fanciers keep adding them to the rearing food. The basic essentials of a rearing food are that parent birds will eat it, feed it to their youngsters and the young will grow well and thrive. Should any of these essentials not be met, then by all means change the rearing food.

For over twenty years I have used brown wheatgerm, bread and milk as a rearing food for Zebra Finches, and it has invariably produced good results. The best way of preparing this food is to crumb the required quantity of dry bread in a food processor or blender and allow it to stand in an open bowl for about eight hours. This allows the bread to dry out and permits better absorption of the milk. The milk should be added gradually and stirred into the bread, using a fork, until the mixture is just crumbly moist. Bread and milk must not be excessively sloppy and the milk added should be totally absorbed into the bread. This mixture can then be given to the birds in small pots once or twice a week prior to the breeding season. When birds have youngsters to feed, it should ideally be given twice daily, and the amount to be fed judged by the quantity eaten on previous days. Obviously, as the youngsters grow, greater quantities of the rearing food will be consumed. Some birds will rear almost exclusively on bread and milk, while others will feed their youngsters with a combination of hard seed and rearing food. Unfortunately, bread and milk can be a rather messy food and is often scattered about by the birds, becoming stuck to the back and sides of breeding cages where it dries as hard as cement. However, if the bread is crumbed quite finely, using the method described above, this problem will be greatly reduced.

Some concern has recently been expressed over the use of milk as a food for birds, especially with regard to their inability to digest lactose. From my own personal experience, I can say that my Zebra Finches have never suffered any ill effects whatsoever by eating bread and milk and I have been more than happy with the health and vigour of young birds reared on this food. There may also be some worry about the milk turning sour during the day. Zebra Finches have a particularly robust digestive system and can cope with this quite easily. Birds are also capable of deciding not to eat food which tastes unpleasant, providing they have the option of other foods available to them. Moreover, when milk is consumed, the first action of the digestive system is to sour it so that it can be digested. All in all, wheatgerm bread (this contains more protein than other breads) and milk is an excellent food in nutritional terms, so provided the parent birds will eat it and feed it to their young, there is no reason why Zebra Finches reared on this food should not reach their full potential.

In addition to bread and milk, I also provide a basic rearing food which is prepared simply by adding a little water to make it crumbly moist. My particular preference is for a food which mixes well with water and does not form a sticky lump when a little too much water is added. Ideally, I like a food which will be of the correct consistency when one part water is added to two parts' rearing food. Some of the more modern concentrated foods will reach their ideal consistency when one part water is added to four parts' rearing food. This always seems to be too dry to me, but these foods have produced excellent results for many other fanciers. When adding water to any of these foods, it should be done gradually, stirring the mixture continually. I know a fancier who adds water to one of the concentrated types of rearing food, using a pressure spray containing clean luke-warm water to get exactly the desired consistency.

There are no hard and fast rules as to which rearing foods are best, the suitability of a rearing food can only be measured by the breeding results obtained when using it. An old maxim is: 'If your method works – stick to it.' I believe this is particularly sound advice and all birdkeepers should always bear it mind. Several very successful fanciers use much more complicated rearing foods than have been outlined here. Most are based on basic rearing foods, to which various items, such as finely chopped hard-boiled eggs, glucose, powdered baby milk, assorted breakfast cereals and vitamin preparations are added. I doubt whether it is necessary to go to these lengths in order to provide a suitable rearing food for Zebra Finches, but it obviously produces good results, otherwise fanciers would not bother to make up these very complicated preparations. Should it be decided to change the type of rearing food provided for your birds, remember this cannot be accomplished overnight. Birds must be given a chance to develop a taste for new foods prior to the breeding season, so that they will take to it readily when there are youngsters to feed. All rearing foods need to be removed from cages the day after being supplied, so that they do not become mouldy or musty, and pots used for rearing food must be washed thoroughly before being re-used.

Soaked Seed

Soaked seed can also be provided before and during the breeding season. A number of different types of soaked seed are available commercially and these only require a minimum of soaking before being offered to the birds. It is sufficient to soak this seed for about twelve hours in cold water, after which it should be drained, rinsed and left to stand for another twelve hours before receiving a final thorough rinse in cold water. After the final rinse, soaked seed can either be added to the rearing food or provided in separate pots for the birds. It is not necessary to sprout the seed. As long as it has started the germination process, it will be of benefit to the birds. I have never personally used soaked seed for my Zebra Finches, but I do offer it to my canaries and I know a number of fanciers who use it for their Zebras.

Greenfood

Various forms of greenfood and wildfood can be provided for Zebra Finches. Suitable greenfoods include cabbage, Brussels sprouts, watercress, mustard cress, lettuce, spinach, dandelion leaves and chickweed. Root vegetables, such as carrots, turnips and swedes, can also be offered in grated form. Many wild seeds are suitable as supplements to the basic diet, with all forms of small seeding grasses, greater plantain seed spikes, meadow sweet, nipplewort seed, seeded chickweed, persicar-

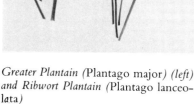

*Greater Plantain (*Plantago major*) (left) and Ribwort Plantain (*Plantago lanceolata*)*

*Nipplewort (*Lapsana communis*)*

ia and knot grass generally being the most popular. When gathering wildfood, it is important to ensure that the collected material has not been treated with harmful chemicals or fouled by dogs and cats. Equally, wild plants growing by the sides of busy roads are bound to be contaminated by exhaust fumes from passing vehicles and, naturally, these will be harmful to your birds. If there is any doubt over the soundness of any supply of wildfood, it is best left alone. It is prudent only to use food which has been gathered personally. A bag of wildfood collected by a well-meaning friend may be contaminated, and the best course of action is to accept the gift graciously and discard it later. Zebra Finches can have rather conservative eating habits. Many will be reluctant to try new foods and often it seems the effort of collecting and providing these items is totally unappreciated. However, Zebras kept in mixed collections will sample virtually any food once they have seen it being eaten by other birds. Any of these foods which are enjoyed by your birds can be provided whenever available,

32

Persicaria or Redshank (Polygonum persicaria) *(left)* and Knotgrass (Polygonum aviculare)

Meadow Sweet or Queen of the Meadows *(*Filipendula ulmaria*)*

Shepherd's Purse (Capsella bursapastoris) *(left)* and Chickweed (Stellaria media)

All of these plants have seeds which are popular with many cage and aviary birds and when in season they may be appreciated by some Zebra Finches

33

although I have reservations about supplying greenfood and wildfood during the breeding season, as it will, more often than not, be used as nesting material. Uneaten perishable foods, such as leaves, should be removed within forty-eight hours, before they start to decay.

Live Food

In the wild Zebra Finches probably eat live food, in the form of insects and grubs, when they are breeding. However, it is quite unnecessary to provide live food for Zebra Finches in captivity. They will breed quite well without this additional food supply, although it can be offered if desired. Naturally, when feeding wildfood, this will often contain small insects which may well be eaten by the birds. Certainly it is a lot of extra work providing live food for birds and one should always leave enough time to enjoy the birds, rather than spend all your spare moments collecting and preparing food.

With regard to feeding birds I would advocate moderation in all things. It is quite easy to get too much of a good thing and more often than not this proves to be harmful. At the present time it seems that diets which are excessive in certain items and totally devoid of others, are being advocated, not only for birds, but also for humans. Within a few years these unbalanced diets are found to be quite unsuitable and the virtues of another system are extolled. At the moment all dairy products and fats seem to be taboo for humans, but to eliminate these totally from our diet would be foolish. With birds, there are also fads and fancies which come in and out of fashion, new wonder seed mixes, marvellous new rearing foods and super new tonics. For many years Zebra Finches have been kept and bred simply by providing good wholesome food and this will continue to be the case in the future. It should be the aim of birdkeepers to find a well-balanced diet which fulfils the requirements of the birds and is relatively easy to prepare. Once such a diet has been found, a great deal of thought should be given before making changes. Mistakes can produce long-term detrimental side effects, remedial action is often impossible and, providing your birds are already fit and healthy, changes can, at best, produce only marginal improvements.

4 General Management

In addition to providing birds with a suitable diet and adequate accommodation, good general management is probably one of the most important aspects in keeping birds fit and healthy. There are a number of chores which need to be performed regularly; failure to do so will usually result in disappointment. Often birdkeepers look for complicated scientific reasons as to why their birds seldom seem fully fit. In many cases, attention to the simple 'basics' of birdkeeping would produce the desired results.

Hygiene

Cages, flights and aviaries must be kept clean and hygienic at all times and this requires that they are cleaned out regularly. It will usually be necessary to clean cages once a week throughout the year, with the possible exception of the breeding season, when this may disturb nervous birds. Old floor coverings used on cage bottoms must be removed, the cages and trays scraped clean and fresh floor coverings provided. Various different materials can be used to cover cage floors; sand, sawdust or paper are most commonly used, but cat litter and other similar products may, in some instances, be more convenient. When using sand or sawdust, it is important to ensure these have not been contaminated by any toxic chemicals such as oil and creosote, etc. Natural sand is probably the most beneficial floor covering as it provides an extra source of minerals and trace elements for the birds. Sawdust is more absorbent, tending to keep cages drier, and therefore the birds cleaner. Paper is ideal when birds are kept in the home, as sand and sawdust are scattered liberally outside the confines of the cage by the birds flying to and fro. Either decorators' lining paper or old newspapers, cut to size, are quite suitable for this purpose.

In addition to cleaning the cage itself, perches should also be scraped clean on a regular basis. When using natural twigs as perches, it is wise to replace them with fresh ones about every six months. If dowel perches are used, these should be washed very thoroughly two or three times a year. A simple method of washing perches is to soak them in water containing a biological detergent, for about twelve hours, remove them, rinse thoroughly and wipe clean, before soaking for a further twelve hours in clean water to remove any traces of the detergent. After the perches have been allowed to dry, they can be replaced in the cages. Obviously, not all the perches can be cleaned at the same time, as birds cannot be expected to sit on the floor for a couple of days while perches are being soaked. Any perches which become smooth and slippy should be roughened with coarse abrasive paper to enable birds to perch securely. Loose perches which fall down continually must be replaced or modified, as they should always be a good secure fit.

All food and water pots must be kept clean and should be washed out regularly. Algae should not be permitted to build up on the sides of water containers, and seed pots should be emptied regularly and the contents sieved thoroughly to remove small particles of dust and dirt which collect in the bottom of the pots. Nest boxes need to be scraped clean and washed in a solution of mild disinfectant after use, before being stored away until the following breeding season.

Maintenance

At least once a year, and ideally twice a year, cages which are not made from laminated boards will need to be repainted. Naturally birds should not be allowed to come into contact with wet paint and will require alternative accommodation. Cages to be painted must be washed out thoroughly, with a mild solution of disinfectant, and allowed to dry. White emulsion paint is most commonly used for cage interiors, but any pastel shade desired can be used, so long as it is non-toxic paint. I have found with emulsion paint, that if a paint pad is used, this is a great help in painting cage interiors quickly and effectively. These pads are generally available from D.I.Y. stores and consist of a foam sponge pad on a stiff plastic backing. If cage fronts require renewing or repairing, this should be done when the cages are being repainted.

Indoor flights will require cleaning about once a fortnight and, again, all old floor coverings must be completely replaced. Sand or sawdust is usually the best material for this purpose. Flights will need repainting at least once a year and all perches require regular attention to keep them both clean and secure. Outdoor aviaries should also be maintained regularly. Those with concrete floors will need cleaning about once a month; gravel floors will require raking every two or three weeks, and natural earth floors should be dug over at least twice a year. All exterior woodwork should be treated with wood preservative once a year to keep the timber in good order, remembering not to allow birds access to freshly treated wood until it has dried thoroughly. Birdroom roofs will need to be inspected to make sure the roofing felt is secure and in good order. It only needs a small tear for water to start leaking into a birdroom, and should this occur, damp and rot will set in. Birdrooms should be kept neat and tidy at all times and this will help greatly in the efficient management of daily duties, allowing more time to look at and enjoy your birds.

Observation

Time should be taken every day simply to look at all your birds. It is very easy, especially when rushed for time, to refill seed and water pots without paying any attention to the birds themselves. This can lead to problems being overlooked until they become more serious and, consequently, more difficult to solve. Any birds which look uncomfortable or unhappy should be caught up and examined. They may have been fighting with other birds, which has prevented them feeding properly, or may simply have a seed husk stuck to their foot, making perching uncomfortable. Birds that are off-colour should be placed on their own. If their condition deteriorates, further action will be required. Any birds which have dirty claws need to be caught up and their feet bathed gently in warm water until clean.

Mites

All birds should be treated with an anti-mite preparation, either in spray or powder form, according to the manufacturer's instructions, once every six months.

For the beginner, it may seem quite complicated to remember all the things which must be done on a daily or weekly basis to give birds the best chance of remaining fit and healthy. However, by adopting a set routine of doing the necessary tasks in the general management of your birds, it will soon become second nature. Remember it is the birdkeeper who chooses to keep birds, not the birds who choose their keeper. Anyone making this choice automatically becomes obliged to give his or her charges the best care possible. In the vast majority of cases, Zebra Finches which are managed carefully and sensibly will reward their owners with nests of fine healthy youngsters and provide countless hours of enjoyment.

5 Breeding

There can be little doubt that the willingness of Zebra Finches to breed in both cages and aviaries is largely responsible for their popularity. The vast majority will attempt to breed given very little encouragement and a high percentage will successfully rear youngsters to maturity. This does not mean, however, that all Zebra Finches will breed; some are naturally poor parents, and others, especially pedigree birds, can be quite fussy as to the conditions they require. In this chapter I will deal mainly with cage breeding, as this method offers the most effective use of space and also allows the mating of specific individual birds. For most people it is not sufficient simply to breed Zebra Finches, the desire is to breed exhibition-quality birds, new mutations or unusual combinations of the established colours. In order to have the best chance of achieving any of these ambitions, it is generally essential that specific breeding pairs are selected, rather than the birds being allowed to choose their own partners at random.

Hen Zebra Finches will lay eggs throughout the year, whether they are with a mate or not. Just because hens are laying the occasional egg, it does not mean that they are in breeding condition. Zebra Finches have an amazing ability to produce eggs and the appearance of odd eggs from time to time should not be cause for concern. Provided the birds are being given a good supply of calcium and adequate vitamin D in their diet, hens which have been laying 'out of season' are quite capable of producing more than enough eggs when the breeding season commences. Eggs laid out of season should be removed from stock cages or flights as soon as possible, to prevent any chance of them being broken and hens developing a taste for raw eggs. Once a bird has become an 'egg eater', it is a habit very difficult to remedy. From a stock of about twenty-four breeding hen Zebras, I would expect to discard, annually, between 100 and 200 eggs which have been laid outside the breeding season.

When keeping Zebra Finches in a controlled environment, such as a heated birdroom, they will attempt to breed at any time of year. Consequently cocks and hens should be kept in separate cages or flights, except for exhibition purposes, when you do not wish them to breed. Although Zebra Finches have been known to breed in quite cold conditions, it is always advisable to maintain a minimum temperature of 10°C (50°F), if at all possible, when the birds are breeding. Usually it is easier to breed birds during spring and early summer, however many exhibitors mate birds so that youngsters can be rung as soon as the current year close rings become available. In Britain these are issued just after the start of the new year and therefore many pairs are put down to breed during December. The main reason for making an early start is to produce youngsters that will be a little bit older and, it is hoped, better developed come the show season.

When breeding in winter, not only does the temperature need to be controlled, the birds will also require about fourteen hours of daylight during which they can feed their youngsters. On damp miserable days, it may be necessary to leave the lights switched on all day. Naturally, if the breeding season gets off to a bad start, any possible advantage is lost immediately and therefore it is essential to prepare birds properly before commencing breeding. It is foolish to pair your birds up simply because another fancier who lives nearby has already starting breeding. Conditions and diets within different birdrooms may vary considerably and the birds within them can also be in very different states of physical health. Personally, I prefer to start breeding from Zebras in February or early March, as I believe the first round has the potential to produce the strongest, fittest and healthiest chicks, which makes it essential that the breeding season gets off to a good start.

Breeding Fitness
Given that the birds are already in reasonably good physical condition, Zebra Finches can be brought to full breeding fitness within about six weeks. Diet control is the main

method used to assist birds in attaining breeding condition, although increases in the hours of daylight and birdroom temperature will also be of assistance. The main addition required to the normal diet, in order to bring Zebra Finches into breeding fettle, is vitamin D. As this vitamin can be obtained directly from sunlight, and because Zebras occur naturally in a warm sunny climate, it stands to reason that it can be lacking in birds housed indoors in cool temperate climates, during the winter months. Vitamin D is required by birds so that they can absorb calcium for the purposes of egg production and it also helps to promote strong healthy bone development in youngsters.

In order to provide additional vitamin D for my Zebras, I use cod liver oil which is mixed into their normal seed diet of millet and small canary seed. The birds are given cod-liver-oil-treated seed for three days, and then untreated seed for three days, alternately, for a period of six weeks. On completion of this conditioning period, the majority of birds are full of vigour; cock birds will be continually displaying, with the hens calling in response and often seen sitting to be mated.

The method of preparing cod liver oil seed is to take the quantity of seed which will be eaten by the birds over a three-day period and add to this cod liver oil in the ratio of one teaspoonful to each pint of seed. This is then mixed in thoroughly and left to stand overnight. The prepared cod liver oil seed is then fed to the birds until completely used and, once untreated seed has been fed for a further three days, a fresh batch of cod liver oil seed is mixed and used as previously described. It is important that containers used to store treated seed are always washed out thoroughly after each batch has been used. Having completed the six-week conditioning period, the birds are given untreated seed for seven days before being paired together. When Zebra Finches become too fit they will often be more interested in mating and nest building than they are in sitting on eggs and rearing youngsters, and this 'cooling off' period serves to take a slight edge off the condition of the birds.

Although many multivitamin preparations can do the same job as cod liver oil, I prefer cod liver oil for two main reasons. It is possible to administer overdoses of vitamins, especially when dealing with small birds, and this can have harmful side effects. Cod liver oil is a natural product and is much less concentrated than the more modern multivitamin preparations, therefore overdosing is much less likely. Also, because Zebra Finches can live for several days without drinking, a water soluble additive can be avoided by the birds if they dislike the taste. However, all Zebra Finches must eat seed regularly and cannot avoid a conditioner which is present in their seed. Critics of cod liver oil often claim that very little is absorbed into the seed and, as Zebras shell all seed before it is eaten, the birds derive very little benefit. The birds will, of course, consume cod liver oil simply by shelling the treated seed and it must be remembered that because they are such small creatures, only very small amounts are required.

My main criticism of cod liver oil would be that it can turn rancid, but, in fairness, if one adopts the basic rules of hygiene, as we all should do when keeping birds, this will never be a problem. It is wise to buy just sufficient cod liver oil to last for one season, rather than a large bargain size which could last for several seasons. The beneficial properties of many preparations become impaired with the passage of time, the action of light and exposure to the air. These factors can weaken the effective strength of the preparation being used, which will then have less than the desired effect on the birds. Of course there are many fanciers who do use multivitamins successfully and dosages should be calculated on the basis that the weight of a Zebra Finch is about 20g.

In addition to cod liver oil seed, birds are also given rearing food about twice a week, two options being provided, wheatgerm brown bread and milk, and also a proprietary brand of rearing food mixed with a little water. In the majority of cases, I have found the birds prefer the rearing food prior to breeding, but once there are youngsters to feed they will favour the bread and milk. Wheatgerm bread, although not necessarily high in fibre, is a good source of protein. While high-fibre bread may be recommended for human consumption, it is the protein content that is required by growing baby birds. Wheatgerm bread also contains vitamin E, known as the fertility vitamin, which is believed to be destroyed by excessive levels of vitamin D. The only other 'conditioners' provided are the occasional green vegetable leaf, an ample supply of grit, cuttlefish bone, powdered cuttlefish and crushed, domestic hens' eggshells, and being allowed to take a reasonable amount of exercise. Prior to the breeding season birds are housed in groups of six to eight individuals, in flight cages measuring between 4ft (1.2m) and 6ft (1.8m) in length. Some Zebra Finches will be very quarrelsome, especially when in breeding condition, and it may be necessary to house these birds separately to prevent excessive fighting.

Pairing

When pairing up birds I much prefer to put all the pairs down at the same time. This gives every bird a mate and helps to eliminate the problem of birds which have pair-bonded by voice prior to the breeding season, calling to one another. Providing all the cock birds are given a mate of their own, most will soon forget about the birds in the other cages and settle down with the hen that has been selected for them. Spare birds are removed from the breeding room and placed where they cannot be seen or heard by other birds.

Nest Boxes

It is usual to provide nest boxes as nesting sites for Zebra Finches and these can be made from plywood offcuts. The most common design is a cube about 6 × 6 × 6in (15 × 15 × 15cm) with a removable top which allows for easy inspection of eggs or youngsters. Various types of entrance can be provided, the simplest being a 2–2½in (5–6cm) gap at the top of the front, across the full width of the nest box. Small holes, about ¹/₈in (3mm) in diameter, should be drilled through the bottom of the nest box to provide ventilation and control the humidity.

Before placing nest boxes in the breeding cages, they will need to be treated with an anti-mite aerosol spray and must also be well filled with nesting material, such as dry grass and moss. Failure to have the nest box well filled often leads to birds building sandwich nests, where the first clutch of eggs is laid and then covered with grass and another clutch of eggs, which in turn is covered with more grass and more eggs. The result is plenty of eggs but very few youngsters. Synthetic products should not be used for nesting material as these can become caught around the legs of parent and young birds, causing permanent injury. Nest boxes are usually placed

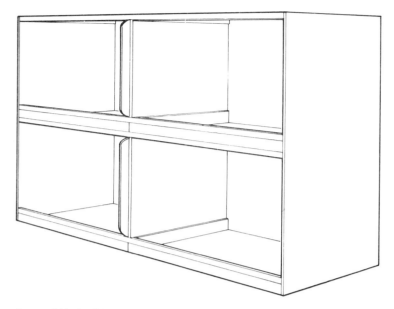

A typical block of four breeding cages, shown with the wire cage-fronts removed

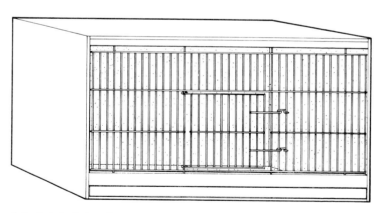

A typical single breeding cage suitable for a pair of Zebra Finches

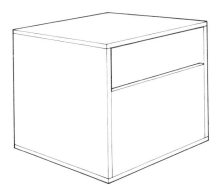

Typical nest box suitable for Zebra Finches

A typical nest box for Zebra Finches, which should be well filled with nesting material, as shown

inside the cage and fastened by means of a small round-headed screw which can be removed easily whenever it is necessary to take out the box. The box entrance generally faces the opposite end of the cage to that to which the box is fastened.

I always provide two perches in each breeding cage, so that the birds may inspect the box initially without actually having to alight on it directly. It is most unusual for a pair of breeding-fit Zebras not to occupy their nest box, although some may require a few minor adjustments before being totally satisfied. Some birds will start to build a nest on top of the nest box, but this problem can usually be successfully countered simply by removing the lid of the nest box completely. Others may try nesting in the corner of the cage, and in such cases the nest box will need to be placed on the floor of the cage, on top of the nesting site chosen by the birds, and the nest box lid may need to be removed.

45

General Care

When putting pairs together, various practices, such as introducing cocks to hens, or hens to cocks, are often advocated, but personally I have never found this to make any difference. Any birds with overgrown, or very sharp, claws should have them trimmed at this time. Long claws can damage eggs or even catch on small chicks, dragging them from the nest. Claws are easily trimmed using a pair of sharp scissors, taking care to leave about 3mm of nail beyond the end of the vein which is visible within the nail. Sharp claws can be blunted using a fine emery board.

All being well, about seven days after the birds have been put together, the first eggs should be laid. Because Zebra Finches are particularly disposed to covering their eggs, and even small chicks, with pieces of surplus nesting material, any unused dry grass or moss should be removed from the breeding cage as soon as laying commences. I also stop providing any form of greenfood at this time, as, more often than not, it is used as nesting material rather than being eaten.

Some hens will lay sooner than seven days after being paired up, and there is a chance that their eggs will be infertile. However, it is best to check all eggs for fertility before discarding them. Eggs laid only three days after pairing Zebra Finches together have, on occasions, proved to be fertile. Sitting usually commences when the third egg has been laid, and once the eggs have been incubated for five full days, they can be checked for fertility. This is simply done if you are able to handle eggs without fear of dropping or cracking them. When a fertile egg is viewed against a reasonably bright light, red veins can be seen starting to develop within the egg; if the egg is infertile, it will be clear or have a slight yellowish tinge. Should eggs show no signs of 'turning' (being fertile) after being incubated for seven full days, they can be discarded and the parent birds allowed to go to nest again. In the majority of cases the next clutch will prove to be fertile. Discarding clear eggs before the full incubation period has elapsed will have no adverse effects on Zebra Finches, provided adequate vitamin D and calcium are included in their diet. Some hens will start to lay a second clutch before the first has hatched and it is best to remove excess eggs if there are more than eight eggs in a nest at any one time. When clutches become too large, it is

A pair of Normal Pieds mating

possible that some eggs will not be incubated properly and this can result in eggs failing to hatch. The most recently laid eggs should be removed, leaving the original clutch intact.

Zebra Finch eggs usually hatch after twelve days' incubation, but, on occasions, hatching may take up to fifteen or sixteen days. While eggs are being incubated, and also when there are small youngsters in the nest, I usually inspect nest boxes twice daily. However, if a pair are seen to be sitting and are reluctant to leave the nest, I will not disturb them provided I am confident that all is well. Some cock birds will try to unsettle hens while they are sitting, and in such cases the cock can be removed for a day or two and then returned to the breeding cage. When he returns, the hen will usually stand no nonsense and be in charge of the situation. If both birds of a pair are seen not to be sitting, the nest box should be inspected. Occasionally eggs will be found covered with nesting material which should be carefully removed in the hope that the birds will go back and recommence incubation. Even if they do return, it could be too late as the embryos may have died.

A clutch of six Zebra Finch eggs, with the first chick to hatch just emerging from the egg

Once fertile eggs have been chilled for more than a few hours after 'turning' there is little chance they will hatch even if incubation is continued by placing the eggs under another pair. Nervous birds may seem never to be on the nest. To test if they are in fact incubating, the eggs should be touched lightly with the back of your fingers. If they feel warm then all is well. It is unwise to spend too much time in the birdroom during the breeding season if your birds are nervy. Personally I do not clean out cages while birds are sitting or when they have very small youngsters, as this disturbance can unsettle breeding pairs.

Rearing food should be provided on the evening before eggs are due to hatch and thereafter twice a day, if possible, until the young are able to crack seed for themselves. Hatching time can be one of the most critical stages of the breeding season, with some parent birds refusing to feed their young. This is especially common in nests where the young hatch on successive days, rather than when two or three young hatch on the first day. It seems as if the parent birds are waiting for more youngsters before they will start to feed. The result is that by

Three one-day-old Zebra Finch chicks

the time the second chick hatches, the first has died, and then the second dies before the third has hatched, and so on until all the young have hatched but none are alive. One possible remedy to induce parents to start feeding is to take a slightly larger youngster from another nest and place it with the unfed chick. The larger chick will beg more vigorously than the unfed youngster and often the parents will start feeding. Newly hatched chicks can survive for up to twenty-four hours without feeding and only require a very small quantity of food for the first day. If larger youngsters are not available, then single youngsters from a number of different nests may be put together in one nest box and given to a pair of birds which previously had just one chick. The eggs from that box can be redistributed among the boxes from which young were removed. Naturally, some sort of record will need to be kept as to the movements of youngsters, and if birds of the same colour are put together at such an early age, it will be impossible to determine with any certainty which came from which pair.

It is quite common for hen Zebra Finches to lay eight or

more fertile eggs in one clutch, but it is quite unrealistic to expect any pair to rear this number of young in one round. Once four or five youngsters have hatched, it is advisable to discard the unhatched eggs which remain, or place them in other nests with eggs of about the same age where there may be only two or three full eggs. Generally those nests which contain four or five chicks, all of about the same age, will produce the best fed and healthiest youngsters.

Ringing

All being well, the youngsters will grow quite quickly and, by the time they are eight or nine days old, they may well require close ringing. Close rings can only be fitted to young birds, usually between the ages of eight to ten days, depending on the size of your birds. The method of ringing is to slide the ring carefully over the three forward-pointing toes until the ring is positioned over the ball of the foot. The ring can then be drawn up the leg of the young bird, over the back claw, until it rests against the knee joint. The tip of the back claw will usually be just under the lower edge of the ring at this stage, and it can be gently eased clear of the ring, using your fingers or a sharpened matchstick if preferred. After ringing, the ring size should be tested by trying to pull it very gently back over the foot; if the ring slips off easily then the bird is too small and ringing should be attempted the following day. I have never experienced any problem with parent birds after their young have been rung and it is not necessary to disguise the rings, as is common practice with some other species.

At about two weeks of age young should be feathering up nicely, but, on occasions, parent birds may start to pluck

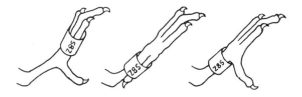

Close ringing a Zebra Finch chick

A seven-day-old Normal Pied Zebra Finch chick

A two-day-old Fawn Zebra Finch chick

A nest of Fawn Zebra Finch chicks at approximately three days old

A ten-day-old Chestnut Flanked White (British) Zebra Finch chick

them. Such a situation is very distressing, but there is little that can be done to remedy the problem. If only one parent bird is responsible, it may be possible to remove that bird and hope the remaining parent will rear the young. Tying a piece of fibrous string to the cage front may offer a diversion to birds prone to pluck their young, but committed feather pluckers can rarely be persuaded to stop the habit.

By the time the youngsters are eighteen to twenty-one days of age, they will usually be ready to leave the nest. Although I believe in inspecting nest boxes twice daily, great care must be taken when the young are about to fledge. A false move may cause the whole nest to scatter and the job of catching the young and returning them to the nest box can be quite difficult.

At around four weeks of age, young Zebra Finches are usually starting to shell seed for themselves and will no longer need feeding by their parents. Some young birds may be a little bit backward when it comes to feeding themselves and they should be left with their parents until they are seen to be feeding properly. It is pointless putting at risk the lives of young birds which are nearly self-sufficient for the sake of a new clutch of eggs. Young Zebras which are not starting to feed for themselves at five weeks of age are unlikely to do so. To go to excessive lengths to save such birds would probably

A nest of Normal and Fawn Pieds, ranging from about sixteen to eighteen days old

A nest of young Normal Zebra Finches at approximately seventeen days of age

53

lead to establishing a strain of birds which had great difficulty in feeding themselves and this is most undesirable.

Often parent birds tend to harry and pluck their first-round young in order to start their second round. In such cases it is advisable to place an extra nest box in the cage for the youngsters. In extreme cases, parent birds may stop feeding their young just a little too soon, and here the only possible course of action is to remove the parent hen and hope the cock will then recommence feeding the young for a few more days until they can crack seed for themselves.

Once youngsters are seen to be independent, they can be taken from their parents and placed together in a separate cage. Although young Zebras do not require rearing food once they are able to eat seed, it is as well to provide a little of this food, twice daily, until they are about six or seven weeks old. It is unwise to put young straight into an aviary or flight as soon as they have left their parents. Most cage-bred birds are at least six or seven weeks old before they are able to be safely housed in an aviary.

Aftercare
When the first-round young are removed, the parent birds should be provided with a clean nest box, once again well filled with nesting material. On inspection of the old nest box, it will usually be found to contain a second clutch of eggs. In the vast majority of cases it is wisest to discard these and allow the hen to produce a fresh clutch of eggs for her second round. Eggs laid before first-round youngsters have been removed are often dirty, damaged, or have been incorrectly incubated, giving rise to a very patchy second round.

When the birds are about to finish their first round, it is advisable to give some additional source of vitamin D for about a week, to ensure there will be no problems with egg laying. Most Zebra Finches will attempt to raise three, four or even five rounds of youngsters in a season, however I never allow any birds to rear more than two rounds of youngsters during one season. It must be very hard work rearing youngsters, and if parents are to be used in the following season, it is wise not to overtax them. Additionally, for anyone interested in exhibiting birds, third- and fourth-round youngsters are rarely as good as the young reared in the first two rounds, and therefore it is unlikely they will make the show team.

Bathing

As time passes, individual fanciers develop their own methods to suit their own birds. One golden rule I employ is never to provide baths for breeding pairs when they have eggs or small youngsters in their nests. When parent birds bathe, they return to the nest with damp plumage and, as the feathers dry, they often become stuck to an egg or to a youngster. As a result, the next time the parent bird leaves the nest box, the egg or youngster is dragged from the nest, with fatal consequences. At one time fanciers were always recommended to provide breeding pairs with baths just before their eggs were due to hatch. This was supposed to increase the humidity and reduce the chances of the young being dead in shell. However, it has been shown that the failure of eggs to hatch is much more likely due to the humidity being too high rather than too low, and therefore the provision of baths during the incubation period will rarely improve the hatchibility. From my experiences of removing the opportunity to bathe from nesting birds, and not just Zebra Finches, I have experienced very little dead in shell (less than 5 per cent even in a bad year) and losses due to eggs and youngsters being dragged from the nest have been significantly reduced.

The most common causes for eggs failing to hatch are poor incubation, eggs having poor quality shells, or embryos being too weak. The two latter problems are generally caused by poor breeding preparation. Poor incubation may be the fault of the parent birds, in which case it should be noticed that they are not attending to their parental duties, or it may be due to night fright. If birds are frightened while it is dark, they may leave the nest and then be unable to find their way back. Where birdrooms are affected by passing car headlights, prowling cats, house lights, or other night-time disturbances, it is advisable to leave a low-wattage light bulb burning and this will enable startled birds to find their way back onto the nest.

Rearing in Flights and Aviaries

Of course Zebra Finches are not only bred in cages, many are reared successfully in flights and aviaries. Usually these are bred later in the year than birds reared in heated birdrooms, and therefore the provision of feeding supplements is not as critical. Nevertheless, birds should be in good physical condition before any attempts are made to breed from them, and it is unwise to pair up birds which are less than eight months of age. When breeding in flights or aviaries, usually several pairs are housed in the same enclosure and it is important to provide ample nesting sites. At least two nest boxes should be supplied for every breeding pair in order to prevent unnecessary squabbling between pairs. Also next boxes should not be positioned too close together; leaving at least 12in (30cm) between each box. Nor should they be placed directly above and below one another.

When estimating the number of breeding pairs to house in a flight, each pair should be allocated approximately 1 cubic yard (1 cubic metre) of space. In practical terms this means an aviary measuring 6 x 6 x 6ft (2 x 2 x 2m) could comfortably house about eight breeding pairs. An aviary of the same size could, of course, house many more individual birds which were not breeding, but because Zebras are so willing to breed, these would have to be either all cocks or all hens.

Zebra Finches tend to breed more readily in flights and aviaries than they do in cages and there can be several possible reasons for this. It may be due to the additional space they are permitted, or to the fact that they are not subjected to the same degree of disturbance in an aviary as they are in cages. Perhaps it relates to the fact that they can select their own mates, or even that birds bred in aviaries are not usually exhibition stock and therefore less temperamental. However, while birds settle more easily to their breeding duties in a flight or aviary, the fact that several pairs are present can lead to problems. Birds may raid other nest boxes in the search for nesting material, causing fighting and disruptions. Young birds, on fledging, can find their way into the wrong nest box, which is bound to cause trouble. In extreme cases, it can result in young birds being killed and eggs broken. Such problems are not easily solved and one must just accept these occurences as being a fact of life when breeding on a colony system. Once youngsters have left the care of their parents and are feeding themselves, they will need to be removed to separate quarters.

Although there is little control over which birds will mate

with which, some birdkeepers will pre-mate their birds in separate cages before allowing them into a flight to breed. This permits mating to take place between chosen birds and the first eggs laid by each hen have a chance of being fertilised by the desired cock bird. Where different colours are being kept in the same flight, intermating between different mutations can produce a large number of visually Normal youngsters. If a pure Normal Pied mates with a pure Normal Penguin, all the young produced will be visual Normals with no Pieds or Penguins being bred. It is unusual for exhibitors to breed Zebra Finches in flights, due to the lack of control, but it would perhaps be possible to start a stud by using birds of just one colour in a flight. The young produced would be of a known genetic colour make-up, but the problem of very closely related birds intermating could be a serious drawback.

When breeding birds, it is important to remember that not every breeding season goes according to plan and even the most experienced fanciers encounter problems. Often the birds are blamed for poor breeding results, but, more often than not, bad results are due to an oversight on the part of their owner. The successful breeders are those who persevere through the bad times and examine their bird management for any possible failings. Should your methods vary considerably from those normally used, there is nothing wrong in this if your birds are breeding well and producing healthy young-sters. All fanciers change their methods from time to time, but changes must be made for good reasons, not just to follow fashion. Whenever anyone suggests changing your methods, it is worth enquiring how many birds this person normally breeds and from how many pairs. It may well be their wonderful new system is producing less youngsters per pair than the methods you already employ. If every pairing used is taken into account, and no more than two rounds of young are taken from any one pair, an average of five to six young for each pair of Zebras, during one season, is a very good result.

Being able to breed your own birds is both satisfying and rewarding from an aesthetic point of view. However, it is very rarely financially rewarding. Anyone who tries to breed birds to make money will generally be disappointed. For the private birdkeeper, the hobby should be taken up for the enjoyment it provides and not with a view to monetary gain.

6 Ailments

The vast majority of Zebra Finches kept within aviculture enjoy fit and healthy lives. The provision of a good diet and the application of sound general management practices will inevitably be the most important aspects in maintaining a healthy stock of birds. However, as with all living creatures, Zebra Finches do from time to time suffer from various ailments and injuries. These fall into two main categories: those which can be treated with simple medicines and careful nursing, and those which require more specialised treatment if any chance of a cure is to be realised.

While simple ailments can usually be treated successfully by birdkeepers, without the need to seek professional advice, more complex problems may never be cured, even when qualified guidance is obtained. Many modern medicines, such as antibiotics, are very strong, and very little research has been done into their use with small birds, so that, often, veterinary surgeons have little practical knowledge of treating Zebra Finches. Attention here is given to the commoner problems associated with Zebra Finches, most of which require only simple treatments.

Hospital Cage

The first aid to the recovery of most small birds is a hospital cage. This is a cage in which the temperature can be controlled by means of a thermostat and it is surprising just how many sick birds will recover when placed in warm surroundings. Before purchasing any hospital cage it is important to ensure that any birds housed in it will be able to extend their wings fully in all directions. This is not for any medical reason, simply a legal requirement as it is illegal in Britain to keep any bird in a cage of smaller proportions, except for the purposes of exhibition. While a hospital cage may be a relatively expensive acquisition, and only used very rarely, fanciers who have purchased such an item, and only used it once or twice, can at least compliment themselves on being very proficient at keeping and breeding healthy birds.

Egg Binding

Obviously this condition only affects hens, but it can be particularly common in Zebra Finches, expecially when birds are kept in unheated quarters, or the local climate is particularly cold and damp. Because Zebra Finches will lay eggs throughout the year, it is not just associated with the breeding season, as is the case with some other types of birds.

Hens who are egg bound will appear very distressed. They usually sit huddled up on the floor of the cage, and the region around the vent is often quite swollen. The cause of egg binding is insufficient calcium and/or vitamin D in the basic diet, making it difficult for hens to pass an egg. While prevention is better than cure in all cases, egg-bound hens can usually be cured quite easily. They should be placed in a hospital cage set to a temperature of about 75°F(24°C), together with seed, water and grit. Initially this may seem to have little effect, but it is the only cure and, in the vast majority of cases, the offending egg will be laid within twelve hours.

The transformation in the egg-bound hen between the before and after state can be truly remarkable and, in my experience, every egg-bound hen treated in this manner has recovered from the complaint. After the egg has been laid, the temperature of the hospital cage will need to be reduced gradually over a two-day period before the hen is returned to her stock cage. Breeding hens which become egg bound should be separated from their mates for about fourteen days and provided with ample calcium-based products, such as grit, crushed eggshells and cuttlefish bone, and also a good source of vitamin D. This can obviously disrupt the breeding season and while hens are laying, if any look slightly uncomfortable, it is a wise precaution to give them additional supplies of vitamin D, often in the form of rearing food, and also calcium sources in an easily digestible form, such as powdered cuttlefish bone.

When a hen becomes egg bound, under no circumstances should any attempt be made to dislodge the egg physically.

Treatments such as oiling the vent, or holding the bird over a steaming kettle, belong to a medieval chamber of horrors, and are not part of a birdkeeper's repertoire. If the egg is broken before being laid by the hen, this will certainly result in the bird dying, so remember to handle affected birds as carefully and calmly as possible. Should a hospital cage not be available, egg-bound birds should be brought indoors and kept as warm as possible, but not placed where they could be affected by harmful fumes.

Chills

Zebra Finches which are maintained in cold, draughty, or damp quarters will be susceptible to chills. The symptoms are quite similar to those associated with egg binding, and treatment is identical to that administered for egg binding, except that birds will require a longer hardening-off period before being returned to their quarters. If birds are continually suffering from colds and chills, then fanciers should take steps to improve the accommodation provided for their birds, or keep a species of bird better able to withstand the conditions provided.

Going Light

Going light is a term used by birdkeepers to describe a condition where birds suffer a severe and rapid weight loss which leaves them in a distressed and lethargic condition. When the bird is handled, the breast bone will feel razor sharp, despite the fact that the bird is eating quite large amounts of seed. Placing an affected bird in a hospital cage at $75°F(24°C)$ will often apparently effect a cure for the condition, but once the birds are returned to their normal quarters, the symptoms usually reappear. The causes for this condition are not as yet fully understood. Antibiotics may be a possible cure, but more often than not death is the result. It could well be that a susceptibility to going light is hereditary and therefore, should birds recover from this disorder, it may be advisable not to use them as breeding stock. Where a number of different birds are affected at the same time by the same symptoms, it is more likely to be due to some form of contagious disease and professional consultation may be necessary. Any use of antibiotics should be given as prescribed by a veterinary surgeon and may well need to be complemented by a vitamin supplement to restore the digestive system of the bird.

Diarrhoea and Enteritis

Disorders of this nature are caused either by keeping birds in unclean conditions, or feeding too much rich food. Affected birds should be kept in a hospital cage at 75°F(24°C), on a diet of plain seed, water, grit and charcoal, and their stock cages, seed pots, drinkers, etc., must be cleaned scrupulously. If birds can be persuaded to take a little powdered kaolin (china clay) in their seed, or cornflour mixed to a paste with warm water, this will help their condition. Should the birds fail to make an improvement within a few days, it is advisable to consult a vet.

Feather Mites

Birds of all species are prone to infestation by mites and one type of mite which can be a problem with Zebra Finches is the feather mite. Infestation by this mite starts with them feeding on the feather, and their presence can be detected by viewing the larger wing and tail feathers against a light source. Should small patches of the feather seem to be eaten away around the central spine of the feather, then feather mites are present. If left unchecked, these will eventually infest the central quills of developing feathers as they breed, and the plumage will be destroyed. Various preparations are available for the treatment of mites, either in an aerosol spray form, or as a powder. These should be administered, exactly to the manufacturer's recommendations, whenever birds are found to be affected, and the dose repeated seven days later in order to kill any new mites which may have hatched from eggs unaffected by the first treatment. Care must be taken to ensure these preparations are not allowed to contaminate food supplies. In my opinion it is advisable to treat all birds for the presence of mites every six months, whether they appear to be infested or not. All newly acquired stock should be treated as soon as possible after being purchased. Two of the most reviled forms of mite within birdkeeping are red mites and northern mites, but, fortunately, these do not seem to attack Zebra Finches.

Scaly Face

This is a condition caused by the presence of a mite which attacks the beak of birds. Its appearance is usually seen as a white or pale-yellowish crust on the beak, close to the plumage around the beak. When the underside of the beak is attacked, it can go undetected for some time unless stock is examined carefully on a regular basis. A proprietary brand of scaly face cream is readily available in most good pet shops and a course of treatment with this will soon solve the problem. If left unchecked the mites will eventually cause the beak to be holed, often resulting in the bird dying as it becomes unable to feed properly. Other treatments for scaly face include applying iodine, or benzyl benzoate cream to affected areas.

Overgrown beaks can be trimmed, using a small pair of scissors, in a similar manner to the way one would trim one's own fingernails.

Sore Feet

Birds with swollen, or sore, feet and legs may also be infested by a type of mite and this can be treated in a similar fashion to scaly face. Any birds with dirty feet should be caught up and have their feet and legs gently bathed in warm water until clean. Overgrown toe nails or claws should be trimmed carefully, using small scissors. When the nails are examined closely, a red vein will be seen inside. This must not be cut, and trimming should leave about 3mm of nail between the end of the claw and the visible start of the vein. If any bleeding occurs, the tip of the claw should be bathed in clear iodine solution to prevent infection and the bird placed on its own until the bleeding stops. Excessively long claws, apart from being uncomfortable, can become caught in wire netting, etc., or damage eggs during the breeding season.

Slip Claw

This is the condition where the back claw curls under the foot instead of being used to grip the back of the perch. When noticed in young birds which have just left the nest, it may be remedied by fastening the back claw to the leg, to prevent it curling under. Split celluloid rings are often very useful for the purpose of holding the back claw against the leg, and it is usually necessary to keep the binding in place for about fourteen days. If, after being bound, the claw again returns to its position under the foot, it is unlikely that the condition can be cured. Even when birds are cured, it should be borne in mind that it may well be a hereditary condition and care must be taken with pairings involving affected birds and their close relatives.

Eye Infections

Birds with sore eyes may have been fighting and squabbling with cage mates, or they may have roosted in a draught. In either case, the affected eye should be gently bathed in a lukewarm solution of boracic powder, usually one teaspoonful to a tumbler of water (dilution instructions on the packet) on a daily basis, until healed. If eye infections persist unchanged after about seven days of treatment, it may be necessary to consult a veterinary surgeon.

Broken or Dislocated Legs

When keeping birds, it is inevitable that sooner or later a bird will damage its leg. Sometimes dislocation can be assisted by very gentle manipulation of the leg, after which the affected bird should be kept in a cage on its own until able to perch comfortably. Where breaks occur, it may be possible, with extreme care and luck, to attach some form of splint, using a spent matchstick, which will need to be kept in position for about ten days. Usually birds will resent any attempt to keep a splint in place, and the only remedial course of action may be amputation. This can be done using a sharp pair of sterilised scissors. The wound will then need to be bathed in iodine and the stump covered with a sterile dressing. Although it can be very upsetting when birds seriously damage themselves, there are plenty of recorded incidents of one-legged birds going on to rear fit healthy broods of youngsters. In order to reduce the chances of birds damaging their legs, all loose ends of wire netting and other similar protrusions should be covered so that birds cannot become caught on them.

Broken or Dislocated Wings

Again dislocation may be assisted by careful manipulation. Breaks, however, cannot usually be effectively treated on small birds such as Zebra Finches. Birds with a damaged wing should be placed on their own and time allowed to be the healer. Some may recover the power of flight, although the wing carriage will almost certainly be spoilt. Birds which do not recover sufficiently to be able to fly again are unlikely to be of any use as breeding stock. Good maintenance of cages and flights will reduce the chances of birds suffering damaged wings.

Fits and Strokes

It is not unknown for birds to take fits. These usually take the form of the affected bird losing the co-ordination of its limbs and therefore being unable to fly or perch properly. In affected hens, fits occur most frequently when they are laying. If a bird takes a fit, it requires no special treatment other than to be left alone. Handling the bird will often make the symptoms worse. Fits are a hereditary complaint and it is wise not to breed from birds with the disorder.

Strokes are also suffered by some birds and, if not fatal, these cause either permanent or temporary paralysis of one side of the body. A bird affected by a stroke should be placed in a cage fitted with low perches and with shallow food and water pots on the floor. Time is the only possible healer and some affected birds may recover sufficiently to lead at least a partially active life.

Antibiotics

Antibiotics should never be given as a 'tonic', they are very strong medicines prescribed to combat specific infections, and it can only be detrimental if they are given except for this reason. There are many general tonics available which are designed to be given on a regular basis. If it is felt that the birds require a tonic, then one of these products should be used. Personally, I feel that birds fed on good quality seed, a little rearing food, fresh water, and ample grit-based products should be quite healthy without needing any additional tonics.

Epidemics

Where a number of different birds are affected by the same symptoms, it is likely that some form of contagious disease is present in the stock. In such cases professional advice must be sought so that the most effective remedy can be utilised.

At times birds will be so ill or badly injured that the only sensible action is to 'put them to sleep'. Should you be in any doubt as to the best method of performing this task, seek advice from established fanciers. It is not a very pleasant job, but, during the past twenty years of keeping birds, it has only been necessary for me to destroy about a dozen birds.

7 Colour Forms

Introduction to Colours

As an aid to describing the different colours of Zebra Finches, their appearance has been laid out in the form of a table. All colours, unless otherwise stated, have red beaks, orangey-red legs and dark eyes. The beaks of hens should be slightly paler than those of cock birds, and it is a fault for hens of any colour to show characteristic cock markings, such as breast barring, ghost cheek patches or flank spots, unless specifically stated.

Although the Z.F.S. colour standards are not laid out in this manner, I hope this method of presentation is easier to follow and provides a clearer and more standardised description. The different colours within the Zebra Fancy have all been derived from the Normal Wild Type or Grey Zebra. Any mutation which had in its parentage anything other than Zebra Finches, would be a hybrid and cannot be regarded as a true Zebra Finch.

The majority of space has been devoted to those colours which are currently recognised for the purposes of exhibition by the Zebra Finch Society. There are many other new colours now being bred, but there is very little precise information on these breeds, making it impossible, at the present time, to formulate an accurate colour standard or permit them to compete against the standard colours.

Normals

The Normal or Grey Zebra Finch is the colour of the species as it appears in the wild. Unfortunately this fact can lead to the belief that they are too common to keep as an aviary or cage bird. In reality, Normals are very attractive birds and if they were rare in aviculture, demand would be astronomical. The variety and colour of markings displayed by these small birds

Feature	Normal Cock	Normal Hen
Head and neck	Dark to mid grey	Dark to mid grey
Back and wings	Dark to mid grey	Dark to mid grey
Throat and breast	Pale grey with black zebra stripes and breast bar	Mid grey
Underparts	White, may be fawnish near vent	Buff
Cheek patches	Dark orange or chestnut	Grey to match breast
Side flanks	Reddish brown with white spots	Grey to match breast
Tear marks	Black	Black
Tail	Black with white bars	Black with white bars

Undesirable Features
Brown shading on wings and back.
Light edges or tips to flight feathers.
General body and wing colour too pale.
Exhibition partners not matching for shade of colour.
Fawnish underparts on cock birds.
Broken or poorly defined characteristic markings.

is remarkable and seldom fully appreciated. In mixed collections of Zebras, many of the other colours lose their appeal unless they are compared to Normals. Although Normal Zebras are generally plentiful, specimens displaying both good type and good colour can be quite scarce and the majority of experienced breeders and exhibitors are constantly searching for quality Normals.

With regard to assessing the colour of individual birds, the first consideration is the head, neck, back and wings. Many Normals, particularly cocks, have colour faults on the back and wings. Instead of being shades of grey, these areas often show brownish shading. The use of Fawns, in the production of Normals, is often blamed for this fault, and birds bred from Fawn x Normal pairings can show excessive brown shading on the wings. However, it is hardly surprising that birds with brown shading on the wings are produced, as the majority of wild Zebra Finches display this feature. Another undesirable colour feature often seen on the wings, is light tips and edges on the primary flight feathers. Again, this fault is present in some wild birds, but with regard to captive stock, it is usually associated with breeding Normals from Chestnut Flanked

A Normal cock Zebra Finch which was successful both on the show bench and as a stock bird

Whites. The means of producing those 'elusive' grey-backed birds may be in part to use Normal x Normal pairings, but also depends on the careful selection of breeding birds and the gradual improvement of stock year by year.

The underparts of cock Normals can also often be faulted with regard to colour. These should be white from the base of the breast bar to the vent, but many cocks will show fawnish shading on their underparts. Again this fault is associated with using Fawns to produce Normals, although many wild birds display the same coloration. Fawnish underparts tend to be quite severely penalised on the show bench in the case of Normals, but, oddly, treated less harshly where Fawns are concerned. Again, there is no instant remedy; it is a case of careful selection and gradual progress. By pairing Normals to

Pieds it will often be found that the colour of the underparts is greatly improved, but such matings would effectively ruin any chance of establishing a stud of Normals.

All the young produced from pairing Normals to Pieds should be visual Normals, but all will carry Pied hidden in their genetic make-up. When these birds are used in future matings, it is usual for birds which show at least one or two odd white feathers to be produced. Such birds are useless for exhibition purposes, as any bird showing errant white feathers must be regarded as a Pied. The most usual areas to display these white feathers are the wings, the tail, just below the base of the beak and the back and sides of the neck. It is possible that birds of this type could be used in conjunction with Pieds for the purposes of producing Pieds, but it is most unwise to mate them to visually pure Normals. The Pied mutation, being recessive, can be carried in hidden form for many generations, and the longer it remains hidden, the worse will be the damage, when it is manifested visually. Usually the presence of Pied will show up after about two generations, but if it does not appear until later, each successive year produces more and more split Pieds. When the Pied eventually becomes visually apparent, it may be impossible to eliminate the split Pieds from your stock without disposing of every bird. Short-cuts may produce good results initially, but they are not the answer to establishing a quality stud of birds.

The underparts of hen Normals should be a buff colour and as this is a basic feature of the species, one could not be expected to breed Normal hens with white underparts. Normal hens which do have white underparts should be regarded with suspicion, as they could well be Normal Pied hens. Generally, Normal hens are of better body and wing colour than cocks. Their most likely fault is to be spoilt by undesirable traces of cock markings.

The presence of breast barring is now the commonest general fault seen in Normal hens and should be heavily penalised on the show bench. The Zebra Finch Society marking standard clearly states: 'Cock markings on hens are definite show faults'. There is a temptation to keep otherwise good hens which show breast barring, as stock birds. After all, the fault will not be evident on any cock birds they produce and it is sometimes thought that hens with these markings will improve the breast barring on cocks. Although cocks do not show the fault, they can pass it on in visual form to their daughters and there is no real evidence to suggest that using a hen with a breast bar will improve this feature in her sons. Indeed, in a wild subspecies of Zebra Finch, where the hen naturally shows breast barring, the cock of the same subspecies has a very poor breast bar when compared to the commoner form of Zebra. Breast barring on hens is a very difficult fault to eradicate and breeders should always try to use birds which do not display this particular feature.

It is always impressive to see a Normal hen which has bold black tear markings and this is a very desirable feature to many breeders and exhibitors. Perhaps the preference for bold tear markings is also partly responsible for many hens, which show traces of breast barring, being produced.

Some hens show ghost cheek patches or ghost side flank spots. Again these are undesirable features and should be avoided if at all possible. Normal hens which are good in other respects, save for ghost cheek patches or flank spots, could possibly be used to mate into colours where these faults would not be apparent, such as Chestnut Flanked Whites. Naturally, a careful record would need to be kept of these matings, as using birds derived from them, in order to produce Normals at a later date, could well result in the faults reappearing in any Normals hens which may be bred.

Unfortunately, there always seems to be a shortage of good Normal hens and this is partly due to the phenomenon that pairs of Normals often seem to produce more cocks than hens. Another factor responsible for the shortage of Normal hens is that when Normal cocks, which are split for a sex-linked colour, are mated to Normal hens, half the young hens produced will, in theory, be visual examples of the sex-linked mutation. Anyone with a surplus of good Normal hens must count themselves as being very fortunate. In my opinion a good unrelated Normal hen is the single most valuable bird when trying to establish a quality stud of virtually every other colour of Zebra Finch.

Normals, particularly hens, can be useful stock birds for breeders of Fawns, Chestnut Flanked Whites, Silvers, Penguins and, occasionally, Pieds and Whites. They allow unrelated stock to be mated into studs of other colours without

A good quality Normal hen is always to be valued in the breeding room

introducing undesirable colour mutations which can compli-
cate pairings. With a little knowledge of genetics, it is possible
to use young birds, produced from matings between other
colours and Normals, to breed birds of the desired colour
form fairly quickly. If a Fawn was used, instead of a Normal,
to improve Penguins, for example, then not only would
Normal Penguins be bred from the split youngsters produced,
but Fawn Penguins could also appear and this may not be
desired.

The fact that Normals are often mated to other colours
naturally means that many carry mutations hidden in their
genetic make-up. While, ideally, one would like to use only
pure Normals when establishing a stud of this colour, in
reality this is quite impossible to achieve. Many top quality

71

exhibition Normals are, in fact, split for other colours. The benefit of using pedigree stock is not so much that they are genetically pure, but that breeders can indicate which colours they may be carrying. Non-pedigree birds are often split for colours which would make establishing a quality strain very difficult.

When hoping to establish a strain of Normals, and sufficient visual Normals are not available, matings to other colours will have to be utilised. The most useful alternative matings are probably Normal x Fawn, Normal x Silver and Normal x Chestnut Flanked White. All of these may have their drawbacks but winning exhibition Normals have been produced directly from such matings.

In my own case, the current stud of Normals, exhibited by my father and me, was founded using both Fawn and C.F.W. matings. A good Normal hen did not have a suitable Normal cock to which she could be mated and was therefore paired to a Fawn cock. From this pairing a number of birds were produced, including two Normal cocks which were, of course, split for Fawn. One of these cocks was mated to an unrelated Normal hen the following year and from their young a Normal hen and a Fawn hen were retained for future use. The Fawn was used as an out-cross for Fawns, while the Normal hen was mated back to her uncle, a Normal/Fawn cock from the Fawn x Normal mating. This mating produced several good Normals, one particular pair being very successful exhibition birds. During the same season, an unrelated Normal cock·was obtained and mated to a C.F.W. hen. This mating produced two particularly good Normal hens. One of these hens was then mated to the best young Normal cock produced from the uncle-to-niece mating and this pairing also bred exhibition-winning Normals. The majority of pairings are Normal x Normal, now that stocks have been built up, but it is intended to use some Dominant Silver x Normal matings as out-crosses in the near future.

Although most of the Normals retained have been bred from Normal x Normal pairings, the original cocks used were split for Fawn, and we have yet to keep a young Normal cock which is not split for Fawn. Selection is done purely on a visual basis, the best exhibition-type birds being retained. In theory, half the cocks produced should be pure Normals and one would expect equal chances of retaining either a pure Normal cock or a Normal/Fawn cock. In fact, all the cocks retained have been split for Fawn; this may just be coincidence, the balance being redressed in future years, or it may be that the presence of the Fawn gene produces an improvement in visual type. This would mean that when birds are selected purely on their visual appearance, Normal/Fawn cocks tend to be retained. Because both Fawn and C.F.W. are sex-linked mutations, it is impossible to breed a Normal hen which is split for either of these colours.

On close examination of the eyes of Normal cocks, some will be found to have a brown iris and others will have an orangey-red iris. It is often thought, within birdkeeping circles, that the orangey-red iris colour shows the presence of Fawn in the genetic make-up of the bird. While there is no hard and fast rule concerning eye colour in the case of Normal cock Zebras, the majority of birds with orangey-red eyes will be split for Fawn, although brown-eyed birds can also be split Fawns. I have seen reference to the fact that wild Zebras have orangey-red eyes, while captive birds have dark eyes, and this is a method of differentiating between the two types. In fact I have owned and bred many Normals with orangey-red eyes, none of which had wild birds in their immediate pedigree.

The use of Dominant Silvers should be sound genetically, as Normals cannot be split for this dominant mutation. There is a feeling that Normals bred from Dominant Silvers may be too pale, but this has not proved to be the case and excellent Normals have been produced from good Silvers. Although Dominant Silvers are not very common, only one or two individuals are needed to establish them within your own birdroom. The birds to look for are those with very little brown shading on the back and wings and these should help to establish purity of colour in the Normals. I would imagine that Recessive Silvers could also produce good exhibition Normals, but there are so few of these birds available that it is impractical to try to obtain them for the purposes of breeding Normals. In the future, Lightbacks may be of use in producing studs of Normals, perhaps being preferred to C.F.W.s, but as yet most of these birds do not have the depth of breeding to produce youngsters of consistently good type.

It should never be forgotten that all the other colours of

Zebra Finch available to fanciers are originally derived from the Normal and, as such, it is the single most important colour. I believe that the future of the Zebra Finch depends on the popularity of Normals and on fanciers being prepared to try to breed good specimens of as pure as possible parentage.

Fawns

The Fawn mutation was one of the first to be established in captivity and is also one of the most visually attractive colour forms. Originally this mutation was known as Cinnamon, as it is sex-linked, and has similarities to the Cinnamon mutation in Canaries. However, the term Cinnamon really refers to a mutation of a bird which normally has a yellow ground colour. Zebra Finches, of course, have a white ground colour and, therefore, it was decided that the term Fawn, already in use for White Ground Cinnamon Canaries, should be adopted.

Fawns are one of the most commonly kept colours of Zebra Finch and are a pleasing addition to any mixed collection of birds. They are sufficiently different to the Normal form to make them of interest to beginners, but, at the same time, have virtually the same depth and colour of markings, therefore retaining the natural characteristics of the species. Fawns differ from Normals visually in that the grey plumage becomes shades of fawn, and cheek patches and side flanks on cocks are a shade lighter. As chicks, Fawns have a paler skin than baby Normals and may be identified at an early age. Being a sex-linked mutation, they can be established in a relatively short space of time, and Fawn hens will often be bred from pairs of Normals.

On the show bench Fawns are undoubtedly the most common colour of Zebra Finch at present. Exhibits in the Fawn classes usually account for at least 25 per cent of the Zebra entry and may be more than 50 per cent of Zebras benched. At the leading all-Zebra Finch shows, it is not unusual to see over 100 pairs of Fawns entered. Apart from being visually attractive, the success rate as exhibition birds also contributes to this popularity. Throughout the history of exhibiting Zebra Finches, Fawns have been leading contenders for major honours on the show bench. In the 1970s they were ousted from their

A Fawn cock, bred during 1983 and winner of several top awards on the show bench

Feature	Fawn Cock	Fawn Hen
Head and neck	Greyish fawn	Fawn
Back and wings	Fawn	Fawn
Throat and breast	Pale greyish fawn with black zebra stripes, breast bar black	Fawn
Underparts	White, may be fawnish near vent	Fawn
Cheek patches	Dark orange	Fawn to match breast
Side flanks	Reddish brown with white spots	Fawn to match breast
Tear marks	Black	Black
Tail	Black with white bars	Black with white bars

Undesirable Features
Unevenness of colour on back and wings.
Light edges to flight feathers.
Exhibition partners not matching for shade of colour.
Fawnish underparts on cock birds.
Broken or poorly defined characteristic markings.

top spot for a time, first by Whites and then by Chestnut Flanked Whites, but lost ground was soon recovered. Naturally, Fawns will not win at every event, but they always tend to push the eventual winners all the way to the line.

Part of the reason for this success lies in the particular type of feather often displayed by Fawns. It seems to be a 'super buff' feather and this enhances the visual type and size of the bird, making many Fawns appear 'cobbier' than Zebras of the other colours. This does not mean that yellow-feathered Fawns cannot be produced, and these may well hold the key to continued individual success with this mutation. The basic colour of Fawns is also an advantage. Being paler than Normals, they tend to hide a lot of marking faults. A Fawn with white-tipped flights will have to be examined closely before the fault is noticed, while a similar fault on a Normal is very obvious. Additionally, because they are both attractive and successful, many breeders specialise in Fawns, and the more birds that are bred, the better are the chances of outstanding specimens being produced.

At one time Fawns were divided into Dark and Light Fawns, and two separate classes were provided until 1961. All Fawns now compete in the same classes, and with the current preference for birds which excel with regard to type (shape), the vast majority of exhibition birds are light Fawns. There are still some quite dark specimens to be seen, but these rarely have the eveness and depth of colour displayed by the true Dark Fawns of the late 1950s and early 1960s. On close inspection, many Fawns, particularly cocks, will be found to lack both evenness and depth of colour on the back and wings, at the present time. Cock birds can often lack depth of colour in their cheek patches and side flankings, especially when compared to a good Normal cock. The underparts of many Fawn cocks may also be faulted as they tend to be off-white, or cream, instead of being pure white. These faults are not, however, glaringly obvious, and birds of outstanding type, which also display these colour faults, are often forgiven their sins on the show bench. Whether this situation is justified may be a matter for some debate, but any changes would be unlikely to affect the success of Fawns for more than a very limited period of time.

Fawn hens tend to show the same marking faults as are

found in Normal hens, these being traces of breast barring, ghost cheek patches and side flank spots. These are just as serious in Fawns as they are in Normals and should be avoided whenever possible. Some Fawn hens will, however, lack sufficiently dark tail barring and tear marks, indeed Fawn hens which have a total absence of tear marks are not uncommon. These should also be faulted on the show bench, although I have seen pairs of Fawns, in which the hens were totally lacking tear marks, awarded specials at very competitive shows. This must be put down as human error on the part of the judge and not a recommendation to breed hens with this fault. I have never bred from a hen which had no tear marks and believe it would be inadvisable to do so. They could, however, be most useful birds for anyone trying to establish a stud of Penguin Zebras, as these do not show tear marks.

It is an accepted practice to pair Fawn to Fawn when breeding exhibition Fawns, but, because it is a sex-linked mutation, Fawns can be mated to Normals to produce youngsters which may be useful in the breeding of both colours. The use of Normals can help to improve colour and also control feather texture in Fawns. While Fawns naturally tend to have coarse buff feathering, too much of a good thing may lead to problems. The continual use of buff-feathered birds will often result in a loss of cobbiness and the apparent size can also be diminished. In order to maintain a stud of exhibition quality Fawns, I believe it is necessary to use some stock birds of a smaller and more intensively coloured type of feather, known generally as yellows, and also to introduce a Fawn produced from Normals about once every three years. When a pure Normal cock is mated to a Fawn hen, Normal/Fawn cocks and Normal hens will be produced. If a Normal/Fawn cock is paired with a Fawn hen, it is possible for Normal/Fawn cocks, Fawn cocks, Fawn hens and Normal hens to be bred. Mating a Fawn cock to a Normal hen will result in Normal/Fawn cocks and Fawn hens being produced. While it may seem unnecessary to put a great deal of effort into trying to breed Fawns of a better colour, it is an advantage, providing good type is also retained. The popularity of Fawns means that their classes are very competitive and any slightly improved visual feature present in the birds can help to place them in front of the competition.

Apart from Normals, other colours are rarely used in the production of exhibition quality Fawns. The only exception, possibly, being Recessive Creams, and their use is very limited due to the general unavailability of these birds. However, they are worth mentioning, as some excellent exhibition Fawns have been produced from Recessive Creams. I, myself, have been lucky enough to possess a few Recessive Creams over the years and these have bred a number of winning Fawns, including birds which have taken Best in Show at All Zebra Finch events. Anyone specialising in Fawns, if offered the chance to buy good Recessive Creams, should seriously consider their purchase, if not for the birds themselves, then because of their tendency to breed quality Fawns. Pairings

An exhibition quality Fawn hen which was successful both as a show bird and as a stock bird

between Recessive Creams and Fawns will produce 100 per cent Fawn/Recessive Cream youngsters, unless the Fawn parent used is already split for Recessive Cream. When two Fawn/Recessive Cream birds are mated together, in theory, this produces 25 per cent Recessive Creams, 25 per cent Fawn and 50 per cent Fawn/Recessive Cream youngsters. Pure Fawns and Fawn/Recessive Creams are visually identical and can only be determined by test matings. Recessive Cream x Recessive Cream pairings cannot produce any Fawn youngsters, only Recessive Creams. Some good visual Fawns have also been bred from Pied x Fawn pairings, but, as in the case of Pied x Normal matings, these are of no long-term use with respect to breeding pure Fawns.

For anyone wishing to exhibit their Fawns, it is important not to allow them into an outside aviary where they have access to direct sunlight. Direct sunlight will bleach the colour and cause the birds to appear very patchy. This patchiness is only temporary and will disappear the next time the birds moult. With regard to the exhibition of Fawns, the most difficult problem encountered will often be matching the colour of specific birds within an exhibition pair. Fawns can show quite a difference in colour shade when viewed together and, in order to bench a good pair, the two show partners must be of a similar shade. It is worth while going through all the stock available, making a note of which birds match with which, so that the most suitable partners can be selected for exhibition. The variation in colour usually becomes less of a problem the longer a strain has been developed. A well-established stud will contain many birds which have similarities in their parentage, and these will tend to 'iron out' the differences between birds. If the correct ground work has been done, the similarities will be good features. When mistakes are made, the similarities appear as the same faults occurring in birds produced from different parents.

The Fawn mutation is often combined with other mutations, such as Pied and Penguin, to produce Fawn examples of these colour forms. These can add variety to mixed collections and, if the good type characteristics of Fawns are retained, they may well be good exhibition birds. Fawn Pieds are exhibited in the Pied classes and Fawn Penguins in the Penguin classes. When combined with Dilute mutations, Fawn produces the colour form generally known as Cream. These tend to be the most popular form of Dilute and, in the future, by combining Fawns and Normal Light Backs, Fawn Light Backs will, I am sure, become a very popular colour.

Fawns are not only visually attractive, they are ideal subjects for newcomers to the exhibition fancy. Because many fanciers specialise in Fawns, initial stock can usually be obtained fairly easily, and there is a choice of sources from which to buy out-crosses when necessary. Wastage, in terms of the number of birds produced that show marking faults, debarring them from serious competition, tends to be quite low. The popularity of Fawns on the show bench may make winning harder, but, by comparing your birds against those of other exhibitors, an accurate assessment of progress towards the 'ideal' can be made. High levels of competition also teach the beginner to accept both winning and losing with good grace. Without this ability very few people can maintain a prolonged interest in the exhibition fancy.

Pieds

A mutation commonly produced in all types of birds kept under controlled conditions is the Pied or Variegated colour form. This manifests itself as random patches of plumage reduced down to the ground colour of the bird, with all other colour pigments, normally displayed in these areas, being absent. In Zebra Finches these patches are pure white, whereas in yellow-ground birds, such as Canaries, they are yellow. Pied birds have always been popular with birdkeepers and will provide added interest in mixed collections of birds. The possible combinations of pied and non-pied plumage that can be displayed by any individual bird are countless, and for the breeder of Pieds the variation in the birds produced from this one mutation can be fascinating. Some birds may have just a few pied feathers, while others appear to be totally devoid of any normal markings whatsoever. Although pairs of dark Pieds tend to produce dark youngsters, and light Pieds usually breed light young, the distribution and extent of the markings is actually quite random. Further variety can be achieved by combining the Pied mutation with other colours, so, in addi-

Feature	Pied Cock	Pied Hen
Head and neck	As other colour forms, but broken with white feathering	As other colour forms, but broken with white feathering
Back and wings	As other colour forms, but broken with white feathering	As other colour forms, but broken with white feathering
Throat and breast	As other colour forms, but broken with white feathering	As other colour forms, but broken with white feathering
Underparts	As other colour forms	As other colour forms, but broken with white feathering
Cheek patches	As other colour forms, but broken with white feathering	As other colour forms, but broken with white feathering
Side flanks	As other colour forms, but broken with white feathering	As other colour forms, but broken with white feathering
Tear marks	As other colour forms, but broken with white feathering	As other colour forms, but broken with white feathering
Tail	As other colour forms, but may be broken with white feathering	As other colour forms, but may be broken with white feathering

Undesirable Features

Exhibition partners not matching for extent or position of pied markings.
Birds showing too much or too little pied markings.
Characteristic markings not broken by white feathering.
Characteristic markings totally absent due to excessive white feathering.

tion to Normal Pieds, breeders can produce Fawn Pieds, Dilute Pieds, Penguin Pieds etc.

With regard to exhibition, Pieds, when selectively bred for several generations, often develop a style of buff feathering which assists in producing birds of good shape and size. Any fancy that includes Pieds in its colour standards has a choice of two options. Pieds can either be allowed to dominate the section by viewing all Pieds, regardless of markings, as equal, or they can be 'controlled' by laying down precise standards as to the 'ideal' appearance of Pieds. The first situation exists within most exhibition Canary fancies where the vast majority of birds are variegated. In some cases classes are provided

A pair of Normal Pieds, very attractive birds in mixed collections of Zebra Finches

for clear birds, ticked birds (which only show a few dark feathers), variegated birds, heavily variegated birds, three-parts dark birds, foul birds (which show only a few clear feathers) and technically marked birds (which show a uniform marking pattern), all of which are different visual forms of the same variegated, or Pied, mutation. It therefore becomes very difficult to acquire birds which are not variegated to some extent, making it virtually impossible to establish strains of non-variegated colour forms. It would be a sad day, despite the visual attractiveness of Pieds, if it ever became impossible to produce self (non-Pied) forms of Zebra Finches. Wisely, the Zebra Finch Society decided to adopt the second option and laid down precise colour standards for Pieds, which protect the other colours from being extensively produced in their Pied form.

The standard asks for birds which are more or less 50 per

cent pied feathering and 50 per cent non-pied feathering and although a little latitude is permitted this is quite difficult to achieve, especially when one considers that the birds have to be exhibited in matched pairs. From the whole spectrum of differently marked Pieds, only a small proportion are regarded as good exhibition specimens. It can be hard enough to breed one 'ideally' marked bird, but, this having been done, it is also necessary to breed a similarly marked bird of the opposite sex before a good exhibition pair can be benched. Careful selection of breeding stock can help to 'standardise' the markings produced in young birds, but there will always be variations in their proportion and distribution. Despite the problems of breeding birds to match the colour standard, some excellent

A Normal Pied cock. Although a little too light, it won a number of awards on the show bench

83

Pieds have been benched over the years, notably during the late 1960s and early 1970s.

Although Pied forms of all the other colours can be bred, Normal Pieds and Fawn Pieds are most commonly seen on the show bench. The darker general colour of these birds helps to contrast the white pied markings, making the birds more

An exhibition Fawn Pied cock, bred by Alf Smith

likely to 'catch the eye' and so be more highly placed in their classes. Silver and Cream Pieds are quite subtly attractive birds and were popular during the early 1960s, but their general lack of success on the show bench meant they soon lost favour. In order to be successful with Pieds, it is usually necessary to breed large numbers of birds so that there will be a reasonable chance of producing matched pairs. It is also wise to concentrate on one colour of Pied, as keeping two different colours effectively halves the possibility of breeding matched pairs. There must be nothing more frustrating than breeding a cock and hen of two different colour forms with identical pied markings because, as Zebras must be shown in true pairs of the same colour, these would be disqualified if benched as an exhibition pair.

The most usual method of breeding exhibition Pieds is to mate two Pieds together: this will produce 100 per cent visual Pied young in the majority of cases. Occasionally a visually pure White chick is bred from pairs of Pieds and the majority of these birds are, in fact, White Pieds. When an out-cross is required and no suitable Pied birds are available, a White Pied may well prove to be the answer. Failing this, a Normal or Fawn of good exhibition type could be used. Because Pied is a genetically recessive mutation, youngsters produced from a pure non-Pied x Pied mating will, in theory, all be visually non-Pied. These young will, however, carry the Pied mutation in hidden form, and when they are mated back to a visual Pied, 50 per cent of their youngsters should, theoretically, be visual Pieds. Providing adequate stocks are available and the birds are not too closely interbred, the policy of mating Pied to Pied, generation after generation, is quite sound, as the mutation is not in any way regressive. Dominant Dilute Pieds can be produced by mating a Pied to a Dominant Dilute and, again, first-generation youngsters should all appear non-Pied. Any Dilutes produced can be retained and mated back to visual Pieds. This will give a 25 per cent chance of producing Dilute Pieds and any non-Pied Dilutes produced will be carrying the Pied mutation in hidden form. If Silver Pieds are desired, then it is best to use Silver x Normal Pied matings, and should Cream Pieds be required, then Cream x Fawn Pied matings are advisable.

Despite the fact that 50 per cent dark and 50 per cent light (or

50/50) Pieds are the most desirable for exhibition purposes; specimens which do not conform to this ideal may well be excellent stock birds. Before discarding excessively dark or light birds, their type and size should be carefully appraised. Any birds which show outstanding qualities, especially with regard to type, could be well worth breeding from in future seasons. Mismarked birds, bred from 50/50 Pieds, can produce a good percentage of 50/50 youngsters. Should these birds also show the good type of the mismarked parent, then real progress will have been made. Generally speaking, darker coloured Pieds often display the best type and these can usually be purchased relatively cheaply, as most people want the maximum pied markings possible for their money and so buy light Pieds.

It is usual for the white feathering on the wings of Pieds to start from the outside of the wing and work inwards, so that the edges of the wings are always white. The actual extent of the white markings shown on the wings will vary from bird to bird. Over the years the wing markings on exhibition Pied Zebra Finches have polarised into two main types, generally called three-quarter wings and saddlebacks. In Britain these terms actually refer to the shape of the Pied markings, rather than to the extent of the markings. On the continent of Europe, birds which are pure white, except for a dark saddle marking on the back and wings, are regarded as a separate colour form, known as Saddlebacks. Future reference in this book to saddleback relates to the interpretation of this term within in the British exhibition fancy. In a three-quarter wing, only the primary flight feathers are pied, whereas both the secondary and primary flight feathers are pied in a saddleback. If a Pied Zebra is viewed directly from above and the dark area of feathering on the wings and back form a V-shape, then the bird would be classed as a three-quarter wing. Should the dark feathering form a semicircular shape, then the bird is a saddleback. From time to time birds are bred that show three-quarter wing markings on one side and saddleback markings on the other. There is nothing to say a bird of this style should be faulted, however it can be difficult to exhibit matched pairs of these 'half-sided' specimens. In general terms three-quarter wing Pieds tend to be a little on the dark side, while saddlebacks are usually lighter, but it is quite possible to breed both

A pair of Normal Pieds which appear not too badly matched in this photograph, but when the birds turn round, below, it can be seen that they are mismatched.

The majority of Zebra Finches can be sexed easily by visual inspection alone, cock birds showing a number of characteristic markings which are absent on hens. On occasions it may be difficult to sex some Pieds but most, including this pair of Normal Pieds, show obvious differences in marking between cocks and hens three-quarter wing and saddleback Pieds to the exhibition standard. Separate classes are not provided for these two types of Pied, but breeders should be aware of their existence and, if possible, avoid benching a saddleback and a three-quarter wing as a show pair.

Ideally, other areas of Pied markings should give the impression that the bird is a 50/50 marked bird, without actually losing any of the characteristic markings or showing them in unbroken form. The characteristic markings are regarded as being the tear marks, cheek patches, throat stripes, breast bar, side flanks and tail. Birds which do not show pied markings on the tail may be excused, as it could be argued that the pied markings coincide with the white tail bars. Absolute perfection would be for 50 per cent of each characteristic feature to be visible, and 50 per cent pied with white, hens showing pied markings which correspond to those of the cock bird they partner. An area often overlooked on Pied hens is the underparts. While cock birds naturally have white underparts and pied markings in this area cannot be easily detected, hens have buff-coloured underparts and these should be evident in a good exhibition Pied hen. This means that the underparts of hens should not be totally white from breast to vent; some areas of the buff-coloured underparts should be visible. Equally hens should also show areas of non-Pied breast plumage, corresponding to the non-Pied markings on the breasts of their exhibition partners.

There are few challenges in the field of breeding type standard birds that equal the problems posed by breeding exhibition quality pairs of Pied Zebra Finches. Anyone who manages to achieve this goal has good reason to be very proud indeed and the search for perfection can last a lifetime. There is, however, some compensation for all breeders of Pied Zebra Finches in the form of the White Pied birds which are produced every so often. These birds tend to display the good type and size of Pieds and have much whiter plumage than genetically pure Whites. While Pieds may be very difficult to match, Whites are the most easily matched colour of all. It is quite possible to maintain a stud of Whites in conjunction with Pieds and the two colours can often be usefully intermated.

Another style of Pied, not mentioned in detail here, does exist and varies in that it has very broken, splashy, "random

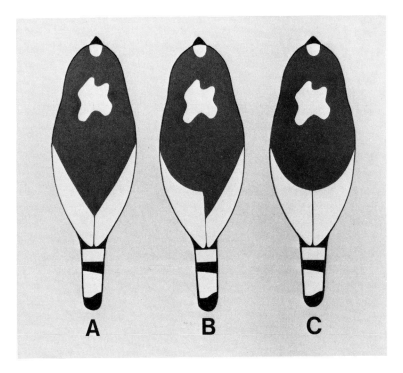

Plan Diagram of Pieds
A: Classic three-quarter wing markings
B: Half-sider: one side three-quarter wing, the other side saddleback
C: Classic saddleback wing markings

white markings. Such birds are sometimes called Grizzle Pieds. The are rarely seen on the show bench, probably due to the fact that trying to breed matched pairs would tax even the patience of Job.

Whites

The White mutation of Zebra Finches is another colour form which made a very early appearance once birds were being bred in controlled conditions. This mutation simply reduces the plumage to white, producing a bird with no colour markings whatsoever, apart from the dark eyes, red beak and

A pair of visually White Zebra Finches, actually White Pieds, which, despite the absence of markings, can be attractive birds

Feature	White Cock	White Hen
Head and neck	Pure white	Pure white
Back and wings	Pure white	Pure white
Throat and breast	Pure white	Pure white
Underparts	Pure white	Pure white
Cheek patches	Pure white	Pure white
Side flanks	Pure white	Pure white
Tear marks	None	None
Tail	Pure white	Pure white

Undesirable Features
Dark flecking or mantling on the head, neck or back.
Insufficient differentiation in beak colour between cocks and hens.

orangey-red legs. Genetically, it is a recessive mutation and should not be confused with Albino which is sex-linked. In addition to affecting plumage colour, Albino also affects colour pigment in the eyes, resulting in pink-eyed specimens. Although an Albino form of Zebra Finch does exist, it is very rarely seen within British birdkeeping circles.

White Zebras are not in any way genetically related to Chestnut Flanked Whites. They are two totally different colour forms and should Normals be bred from two white-coloured Zebras, it is likely that a White cock has been mated to a pale C.F.W. hen. Neither is the White Zebra Finch mutation in any way similar to the Dominant White mutation which, for example, is found in Canaries. This only affects the ground colour of the bird, reducing it from yellow to white, and therefore is not applicable to white-ground birds, such as Zebra Finches. Although it may seem pointless to produce birds which lack the varied and interesting colour markings usually associated with Zebra Finches, White birds can be very attractive and are popular in mixed collections. The pure white plumage helps to accentuate the different markings present in other colour forms.

The original Whites, which were genetically 100 per cent pure White, were often spoilt by showing dark flecking on the neck and back, known as mantling. They also tended to lack good cobby type and rarely featured in the honours on the show bench. However, quite by chance during the 1960s, a number of Pied breeders started to produce a few pure white birds, from their Pieds, which were in fact White Pieds. These birds were largely ignored when first produced, being of little interest to anyone striving to produce 50/50 Pieds. Before too long, however, fanciers realised that these birds actually conformed more closely to the colour standard for Whites than did the genetically pure White birds seen on the show bench at that time. Being pure white, there was no way judges could wrong-class the Pied Whites for being Pieds, even though they were being shown in a non-Pied class. In addition to showing better colour, many had also inherited good type and size from the Pied stock. A few exhibitors started to bench Pied Whites as Whites, and were almost immediately rewarded with success.

At that time Whites were exhibited in the Any Other Colour class, along with Chestnut Flanked Whites and Penguins, at the majority of shows. In 1969, separate classes were provided for Chestnut Flanked Whites, leaving just Whites and Penguins in the A.O.C. Class. This effectively meant that it was easier to win a class with a pair of Whites than it had been previously. Perhaps this fact, coupled with a few pairs having already won major honours at shows, was largely responsible for creating a new interest in Whites. Breeders, particularly those who kept Pieds, made an effort to produce exhibition Whites and within a very short period of time they went through a 'purple patch' with regard to success on the show bench. In the very early 1970s, Whites were regularly in contention for the major awards, by 1972 they seemed virtually unbeatable and when a pair of White Zebras won the Supreme Award for Best in Show at the National Exhibition of Cage and Aviary Birds, at the end of that season, interest was at a peak. For the next two or three years they continued to feature prominently on the show bench, but since that time their general quality and success has declined somewhat.

This decline could well be due to breeders of Whites over-looking how the majority of the outstanding White Zebras were originally produced. Instead of regularly mating Whites to Pieds, White x White matings have predominated. In my view the best way of producing exhibition Whites is to employ the frequent use of Pied x White matings. The markings of the Pieds to be used are relatively unimportant, the feature to look for being good type and, if possible, good size. When the choice is between a dark Pied and a light Pied of the same type and size, it would seem reasonable to choose the lighter bird. However, if the only Pieds of good type available are dark birds, these will usually be quite suitable. Should the first matings between a Pied and White Pied not produce any pure White youngsters, this is no reason for concern. All the young produced will be carrying White in their genetic make-up and the birds which show the best type characteristics can be retained for remating to Pied Whites. It is probably advisable, when specialising in Whites, to also try to establish a strain of good Pieds, so that out-crosses are available when required. Generally speaking, Pied will need introducing into Whites at least once every three generations.

If, when paired together, two visually pure white birds, bred from Pieds, were to produce visual Pied youngsters, it would mean that one, or both, was not actually White in genetic terms. It is possible to produce Pieds which display so much variegation that they appear to be pure white. Such birds, given the other desired features, could be successfully exhibited in the White class, as there is no visual way of categorising these birds. The use of Pieds which appear to be Whites should have no detrimental affect on a stud of Whites – indeed, they could be beneficial.

Good quality Normals and Fawns may also be used as out-crosses for Whites. If these matings are used, remember that any Normals or Fawns produced, in all probability, will not only be carrying White in their genetic make-up, they will also be split for Pied. This means that visual selfs from these matings could cause havoc if introduced into a stud of pure Normals or Fawns. As usual with recessive mutations, first-generation young will, in theory, not show the presence of the recessive mutation in visual form when Whites are mated to Normals or Fawns. The young produced will then usually need to be mated to visual Whites in order to produce White youngsters. In such cases, 50 per cent of the young should be visual Whites, the remainder being split for White. The use of Normals or Fawns would be more of an aid to try to improve type, if suitable Pieds were not available, rather than as a means to improve colour. When Whites are produced from Fawns, these birds should not be introduced into a stud of Normal Pieds, unless it is the intention to produce Fawn Pieds. While Whites produced from Fawn/White x White matings need not necessarily be Fawn Whites, there is a chance that they will be carrying the mutant gene for Fawn. For a breeder of pure Normal Pieds, it could be quite annoying to find 'Fawn blood' had unknowingly been introduced into his or her strain.

Whites are still prone to showing mantling and a few individuals with this fault will usually be bred each season. In some case the dark flecking disappears when the birds moult, and it is therefore important to keep records of birds which have shown mantling as young birds. Obviously, if two apparently pure white birds, which both showed mantling as youngsters, were mated together, there is a good chance that their youngsters will display this fault to a greater extent. Remember that this mantling was not eradicated by pairing White to White, and that the introduction of Pieds was the solution to the problem.

Type is particularly important in Whites as, apart from being of pure white colour, this is virtually the only other exhibition feature they display. While breeders of other colours have to produce birds with fully barred tails, White specialists do not have to contend with these finer points. In order to impress the judge, Whites need to display some feature which is better than that shown by the competition, and really this can only be their type or shape. The Whites which did so well from the early to mid 1970s, excelled for type, and it was this particular feature which elevated them to such prominence.

There is one marking that is required in exhibition Whites and this is the difference in beak colour between cocks and hens. Without this differential, judges may be inclined to think they are looking at two cocks or two hens, and would be quite justified in penalising the exhibit accordingly.

At times, hand-washing birds is advocated when exhibiting Whites. However, unless you are confident of being able to hand-wash birds successfully, it should not be attempted. Hand-washing is not done to get the birds clean; frequent baths and spraying should achieve this. It is done to 'break' the small wax-covered pin feathers shown by birds coming out of the moult, and also to remove natural oils from the plumage, thus enhancing the visual type of the birds. The true art is to hand-wash each show bird just once during a show season and the full benefit only becomes apparent after two or three weeks. Birds which have been hand-washed should be kept in a warm place for at least twelve hours, as it greatly reduces their resistance to cold.

One of the best methods of removing pin feathers is to house birds in pairs, and providing they do not fight or pluck each other, they will remove the waxy pins by mutual preening. As Whites do not have any tail barrings, which may be removed by cage mates, it is much safer to house these in pairs than the other colours.

White Zebra Finches offer ample scope for both exhibitors and non-exhibitors alike. Their numbers may have declined since their hey-day in the 1970s, but it should be remembered that they have reached heights as yet unequalled by any other colour of Zebra Finch. The basic ingredients of those birds are still available to all fanciers and there is no reason why the achievement should not be repeated.

Dilutes

There are three different mutations, recognised by the Zebra Finch Society, generally regarded as being forms of Dilute Zebra Finches. All affect, to some degree, the visual intensity of the colour pigments normally displayed by Zebras, without any characteristic markings being totally lost or altered in shape and extent. Although each reduces the colour slightly differently, the primary difference among these three types of Dilute is in the genetic inheritance of the mutations. One type is genetically Dominant to the Normal form, another is Recessive and the third is Sex-Linked.

Combinations between each one of these mutations, and all other Zebra Finch mutations, can be produced, with the exception, due to a genetic 'quirk', of Sex Linked Dilute Chestnut Flanked Whites. However, because Normals and Fawns are the only colours dark enough to show the effect of dilution to advantage, breeders are mainly concerned with diluted forms of these two colours. It is usual to refer to Dilute Normals as Silvers and Dilute Fawns as Creams in the case of Dominant and Recessive Dilutes. Sex Linked Dilutes are commonly called Light Backs, and while the majority of these currently being seen on the show bench are the Normal form, it is possible to combine the mutation with other colour forms, including Fawn.

At the majority of shows, all the different types of Dilute are exhibited in the same class, but must be benched in matched pairs of the same mutation. A few of the larger shows divide the Dilutes into two classes, one for Silvers and Light Backs and the other for Creams. Should Fawn Light Backs be produced, they will most probably be categorised as Creams for exhibition purposes. Two mutations not currently recognised by the Z.F.S. which are being bred on the Continent, namely Isabels and Agates, would also appear to be forms of Dilute.

The different Dilutes are not generally intermated within the British Zebra Finch fancy, but some unusual and subtly coloured birds can be produced by combination matings. Calculation of colour expectations from the various pairings possible could be rather complicated, and a carefully planned breeding programme, involving several generations, may be needed to produce specific combinations.

Dominant Dilutes

The first Dilute mutation to appear was the Dominant variety, so called because it is genetically dominant to the Normal Zebra. Good Dominant Dilutes, to many fanciers, are one of the most visually appealing colours of Zebra Finch and are particularly effective when kept in mixed collections of diluted and undiluted birds. Unfortunately, many individuals are too dark or of a patchy colour and this greatly detracts from their appearance. Breeders of exhibition birds will find these birds offer a challenge, but many prefer to concentrate on other

A Fawn Pied cock Zebra Finch.

A Dominant Cream cock Zebra Finch.

A Normal cock Zebra Finch.

A Fawn cock Zebra Finch.

A Normal hen Zebra Finch.

A Fawn hen Zebra Finch.

A Normal Pied cock Zebra Finch.

A White (White Pied) cock Zebra Finch.

A Normal Pied hen Zebra Finch.

A White (White Pied) hen Zebra Finch.

A Dominant Silver cock Zebra Finch.

A Normal Light Back cock Zebra Finch.

A Dominant Silver hen Zebra Finch.

A Normal Light Back hen Zebra Finch.

A Chestnut Flanked White cock Zebra Finch.

A Fawn Penguin cock Zebra Finch.

A Chestnut Flanked White hen Zebra Finch.

A Fawn Penguin hen Zebra Finch.

A Normal Penguin cock Zebra Finch.

A Normal Yellow-Beak cock Zebra Finch.

A Normal Penguin hen Zebra Finch.

A Normal Black Breasted cock Zebra Finch.

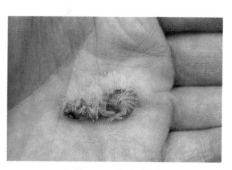

A Chestnut Flanked White Zebra Finch about six hours old.

A Chestnut Flanked White Zebra Finch about twenty-four hours old.

A Chestnut Flanked White Zebra Finch about thirty-six hours old.

Three Normal Zebra Finches all about four days of age.

A Chestnut Flanked White Zebra Finch about six days of age.

A Normal Zebra Finch about six days old.

A Chestnut Flanked White Zebra Finch about nine days old.

A Fawn Zebra Finch about eleven days old.

A Dominant Silver Zebra Finch about thirteen days old.

A Normal Pied Zebra Finch chick at fourteen days old.

A Chestnut Flanked White Zebra Finch at about sixteen days old.

A Normal Zebra Finch about sixteen days old.

A Fawn Black Breasted hen Zebra Finch.

A nest containing six Normal Zebra Finches about four or five days old.

A nest containing five Fawn Zebra Finches about fourteen to sixteen days old.

A nest containing one Normal Light Back and two Chestnut Flanked White Zebra Finches all about eighteen days of age.

A pair of Normal Zebra Finches.

Feature	Dominant Silver Cock	Dominant Silver Hen
Head and neck	Pale silvery grey	Pale silvery grey
Back and wings	Silvery grey	Silvery grey
Throat and breast	Pale silvery grey with grey zebra stripes and breast bar	Silvery grey
Underparts	White	White or very pale buff
Cheek patches	Pale orange or cream	Silvery grey to match breast
Side flanks	Orange or pinkish fawn with white spots	Silvery grey to match breast
Tear marks	Grey to match breast bar	Grey
Tail	Grey with white bars	Grey with white bars

Undesirable Features

Brown shading on back and wings.
General patchiness of colour or general shade of colour too dark.
Exhibition partners not matching for shade of colour.
Loss of characteristic markings due to excessive dilution.

Feature	Dominant Cream Cock	Dominant Cream Hen
Head and neck	Cream	Cream
Back and wings	Cream	Cream
Throat and breast	Cream with pale chocolate zebra stripes and breast bar	Cream
Underparts	White	Cream
Cheek patches	Pale orange	Cream to match breast
Side flanks	Pale orange with white spots	Cream to match breast
Tear marks	Pale chocolate	Pale chocolate
Tail	Dark cream with white bars	Dark cream with white bars

Undesirable Features

General patchiness of colour or general shade of colour too dark.
Exhibition partners not matching for shade of colour.
Loss of characteristic markings due to excessive dilution.

colours where there is less wastage and a better chance of producing exhibition quality birds.

In birdkeeping circles, with regard to dominant mutations, it is often the case that a double dose of the mutation proves to be lethal. Over the years it has been accepted that while the gene responsible for the Dominant Dilute mutation is not, in fact, lethal, youngsters produced from matings between Dominant Dilutes are often weak and lack robust physical health. The practice of always mating Dominant Dilutes to undiluted birds, usually either Normals or Fawns, has therefore become established, and such matings will, in theory, produce 50 per cent diluted youngsters and 50 per cent undiluted young. Undiluted birds bred from Dominant Dilutes do not carry the Dilute gene and, when mated to Dilutes, are no more likely to produce Dilute youngsters than a bird bred from two undiluted parents. In order to breed any Dominant Dilutes, at least one of the parent birds used must be a visual Dominant Dilute. It is impossible for any Zebra to be split for the Dominant Dilute mutation. A Dominant Dilute which carries only one dilute gene is usually called a single factor (s.f.), while birds possessing two Dominant Dilute genes in their make-up are referred to as double factor (d.f.) Dilutes. In practical terms, the vast majority of Dominant Dilutes are single factor birds and, in theory, there should be no visual difference between s.f. and d.f. birds.

Dominant Dilutes are usually the palest form of pure bred Dilute and the mutation affects all the colours and markings normally present in the undiluted form. Ideally, the dilution should produce nice evenly coloured birds which still retain all their characteristic markings, in diluted form, without any being totally lost. The most attractive examples of the mutation tend to be the paler specimens and these are therefore more highly prized than the darker Dominant Dilutes. Specialist Dilute breeders tend to look for Dominant Silvers which are pale silvery grey on the head, neck, back and wings, and Dominant Creams which are very pale cream in these areas. Sometimes pale Dominant Dilute cocks, especially Silvers, are criticised for showing too much dilution in their cheek patches. Providing birds have all the other features desired in good quality exhibition Dominant Dilutes, this criticism is, in my opinion, unreasonable. To severely penalise

A Dominant Cream cock, bred by the late Wilf Parke, which, although only a small bird physically, displayed excellent head qualities

otherwise good Dilutes because their cheek patches are too pale would be very harsh treatment.

When first introduced to Britain, breeders mainly concentrated on Dominant Silvers, but it did not take long before the mutation was combined with the Fawn colour form and this produced Dominant Creams. Dominant Creams have somewhat eclipsed Dominant Silvers on the show bench, and therefore Silvers tend to be less numerous generally. In some ways this is a great pity, as a good Dominant Silver cock must surely be one of the most beautiful of all Zebra Finches. The problem is that very few good, light, evenly marked Silvers are produced; many are too dark, generally patchy, or have

99

undesirable brown shading on the back and wings. With Creams, although it is still not easy to breed light, evenly marked birds, there is usually much less wastage and so a better chance of breeding well-matched exhibition pairs. Dominant Dilutes generally can show a large variation in both the shade of the body colour and also the colour and shade of characteristic markings.

Creams can be bred by mating Silvers to Fawns. A Fawn cock paired to a Silver (s.f.) hen will, in theory, produce equal proportions of Normal/Fawn cocks, Silver (s.f.)/Fawn cocks, Fawn hens and Cream (s.f.) hens. A Silver (s.f.) cock mated to a Fawn hen should produce equal numbers of Silver (s.f.)/ Fawn cocks, Normal/Fawn cocks, Normal hens and Silver (s.f.) hens. When a Silver (s.f.)/Fawn cock is mated to a Fawn hen, some Cream (s.f.) cocks and hens, as well as Normal/ Fawn cocks, Fawn cocks, Silver (s.f.)/Fawn cocks, Normal hens, Fawn hens and Silver (s.f.) hens, may be bred. Nowadays the problem is more likely to be the reverse, that is to say, producing Silvers from Creams. This can be achieved by mating Creams to Normals. A Cream (s.f.) cock paired to a Normal hen will produce Normal/Fawn cocks, Silver (s.f.)/ Fawn cocks, Cream (s.f.) hens and Fawn hens. Mating a Normal cock to a Cream (s.f.) hen can give Normal/Fawn cocks, Silver (s.f.)/Fawn cocks, Normal hens and Silver (s.f.) hens. Many Normal cocks are, however, split for Fawn, and a Normal/Fawn cock mated to a Cream (s.f.) hen would produce Normal/Fawn cocks, Fawn cocks, Silver (s.f.)/Fawn cocks, Cream (s.f.) cocks, Normal hens, Fawn hens, Silver (s.f.) hens and Cream (s.f.) hens, theoretically in equal proportions. When a Silver (s.f.)/Fawn cock is paired to a Normal hen, the possible colour expectations are Normal cocks, Normal/Fawn cocks, Silver (s.f.) cocks, Silver (s.f)/Fawn cocks, Normal hens, Fawn hens, Silver (s.f.) hens and Cream (s.f.) hens.

Actual percentages of the different coloured young bred, can vary considerably from nest to nest and it often seems, when one particular colour is desired, that that specific colour will not be produced. A number of breeders have also experienced problems in rearing young Dilutes to maturity, and this may be due to them having diluted gape markings. When a nest contains both diluted and undiluted youngsters, the

A pair of Normals which were successful on the show bench during 1973. The cock depicted was bred from a Silver x Normal pairing

undiluted birds can create a greater stimulus to be fed by their parents because they have normal gape markings, and this may lead to young Dilutes not receiving their fair share of food.

In order to maintain a good stud of Dominant Dilutes, it is usually necessary to have at your disposal either a ready supply of Normals, in the case of Silvers, or Fawns, in the case of Creams. This means that fanciers would often be well advised to concentrate on either Normals or Fawns and build up studs of these colours, before starting to specialise in Dominant Dilutes. The inherent problems of producing Dilutes which are too dark, or of a patchy colour, can only be combated by careful selective breeding, retaining lighter even-colour birds and disposing of any dark or patchy Dilutes. Careful attention should also be paid to the Normal and Fawn stock used in matings. Any birds which show unevenness of colour will usually be unsuitable for the production of Dilutes. Although other colours, apart from Normals and Fawns, may be used for matings involving Dominant Dilutes, the vast majority of good quality exhibition Dilutes have been produced by pairing either Normals or Fawns to Dominant Silvers or Creams.

In the past, Chestnut Flanked Whites were mated to Silvers in an attempt to breed paler, more evenly coloured birds, and this method has not been totally unsuccessful. Naturally, any C.F.W.s produced from these matings will be of little use for the production of exhibition quality C.F.W.s, as they may well be dilute birds and have an undesired effect on the depth and colour of markings in the C.F.W.s bred from them. I feel there is still scope for more experimentation to be done in mating Dominant Dilute to Dominant Dilute. Not only would this increase the percentages of Dilute youngsters being bred, it might produce more light birds and could also improve the patchiness which tends to be a major problem at present. In the future, intermatings between Dominant Dilutes and Light Backs could produce some attractively coloured birds, although I feel that, in the long term, these birds could once again show an undesirable patchiness of colour. I am sure that this problem stems from using too many buff-feathered stock birds, due to the continual quest for type and size in present-day show birds.

On the show bench, Dominant Dilutes regularly won top awards in the early days and continued to do so until the late 1960s. The 1970s saw a general decline in the numbers of these birds being bred and exhibited and only a handful of major specials winners were benched. During the 1980s, there has been something of a resurgence in their numbers and, consequently, the general quality has once again risen, with Dominant Dilutes taking a number of the top prizes at leading shows.

Dominant Dilutes are a most attractive colour form, well worth the attention of breeders with mixed collections and also those who are specialist exhibitors. They 'knit' well into any stud of Normals or Fawns, providing additional variety and interest in most collections.

Recessive Dilutes

Recessive Dilutes, as the name suggests, are a dilute mutation which is genetically recessive, and therefore has the same

Feature	Recessive Silver Cock	Recessive Silver Hen
Head and neck	Bluish grey	Bluish grey
Back and wings	Bluish grey	Bluish grey
Throat and breast	Silvery grey with darker grey zebra stripes and breast bar	Bluish grey
Underparts	White	Pale buff or very pale grey
Cheek patches	Orange	Bluish grey to match breast
Side flanks	Chestnut with white spots	Bluish grey to match breast
Tear marks	Grey to match breast bar	Grey
Tail	Bluish grey with white bars	Bluish grey with white bars

Undesirable Features
Brown shading on wings and back.
Patchiness of colour on back and wings.
General body colour too dark, showing insufficient dilution.
Exhibition partners not matching for shade of colour.

Feature	Recessive Cream Cock	Recessive Cream Hen
Head and neck	Pale fawn	Pale fawn
Back and wings	Pale fawn	Pale fawn
Throat and breast	Pale fawn with pale grey zebra stripes and breast bar	Pale fawn
Underparts	White, may be fawnish near vent	Pale fawn
Cheek patches	Orange	Pale fawn to match breast
Side flanks	Chestnut with white spots	Pale fawn to match breast
Tear marks	Pale grey to match breast bar	Pale grey
Tail	Pale grey with white bars	Pale grey with white bars

Undesirable Features
Patchiness of colour on back and wings.
General body colour too dark, showing insufficient dilution.
Exhibition partners not matching for shade of colour.

hereditary characteristics as Pieds, Penguins and other recessive mutations. Unfortunately, even though visually quite attractive, they are very scarce, mainly due to many fanciers being totally unaware of their existence. As with other dilutes, the two forms of main interest are Dilute Normals and Dilute Fawns, and again these are referred to as Silvers and Creams.

Apart from the genetic differences between Dominant and Recessive Dilutes, there are visual differences which must be recognised generally if Recessive Dilutes are ever going to become popular. The dilution in Recessive Dilutes only seems to occur in the black pigment of the plumage, therefore markings, such as tail barrings, tear marks and breast barring, are noticeably diluted when compared to the undiluted form. The general body colour is slightly diluted, with any black pigmentation within these areas being reduced, but the areas of plumage which contain very little black pigment, such as cheek patches and side flanks, are displayed quite prominently. The body colour of Recessive Dilutes is usually darker than that of Dominant Dilutes, but tends to show less patchiness.

Recessive Silvers, although very scarce at the present time, were commonly advertised as Blue Zebras during the early 1960s. This name was derived from the bluish grey colouring of their head, neck, back and wings. Any birds of this coloration, entered in the dilute classes, which still retain quite prominent cheek patches and side flanks, are well worth a second look. While they may not be particularly successful on the show bench, my experiences with Recessive Creams would lead me to believe that Recessive Silvers could be very useful out-crosses for a stud of Normals. I am sure a number of these birds are overlooked every season, either because they are thought to be dark Dominant Dilutes, or, if retained for breeding purposes in the belief that they are Dominant Dilutes, because no Dilutes are produced among their first generation youngsters, they are discarded.

I have been fortunate enough to breed and exhibit a few Recessive Creams during my time in the fancy. On first inspection these birds often seem to be pale Fawns, and not until examination of the black characteristic markings is it realised that they are actually Recessive Creams. The first birds of this type my father bred were produced from a pair of visual Fawns and naturally one does not expect to breed

Dilutes from such a mating. As the young feather up in the nest, their plumage often seems to take on a pinkish cast. Once fully moulted out, the intensity of colour in the cheek patches and side flanks tends to rule out the possibility of them being any form of Dilute, but Dilutes they are. As they are genetically recessive, once they are mated back to a Fawn, in the majority of cases all the young produced will be visual Fawns and the mutation has apparently been lost. Not until two birds, which both carry the gene for Recessive Dilute, are mated together is there any chance of young Recessive Dilutes being produced.

Although we have been unable to establish a stud of Recessive Dilutes, they have proved themselves to be very worthwhile birds. Without exception, when a Recessive Cream has been mated to a good quality Fawn, within two generations their Fawn descendants have gone on to win major honours on the show bench. Generally, I have found Recessive Creams, produced from two Fawns, tend to be the best for colour, type and size, while those bred from Recessive × Recessive mat-

A Recessive Cream cock, which, when mated to a good quality Fawn hen, produced excellent Fawns, among them the bird depicted on page 106

A Fawn cock, bred from a Recessive Cream cock (the bird on page 105) x Fawn hen mating. This bird was a member of the pair which won Best in Show at the 1975 S. & N.C.Z.F.S. Club Show

ings have been rather disappointing. At times it may be difficult to differentiate between a Recessive Cream hen and a dark Dominant Cream hen, as they do not show the tell-tale orange markings. This, perhaps, means Recessive Cream hens have often been used in the belief that they were Dominant Creams. As they will fail to produce the expected breeding results, instead of considering the possibility of the hen being a Recessive, the bird is simply eliminated from future breeding programmes.

Should dilutes be bred from two undiluted birds, then they cannot be of the Dominant mutation and must therefore be either Recessive Dilutes or Light Backs. If a Dilute cock is produced, then it is bound to be a Recessive and both parent birds must be carrying the gene responsible hidden in their genetic make-up. When the Recessive and Dominant Dilute mutations are intermated repeatedly, it is possible to breed birds which are a combination of the two mutations and these birds may well be of the desired light, even colour, without showing the excessive cheek patch dilution which is sometimes criticised in pale Dominant Dilutes.

Light Backs

Feature	Normal Light Back Cock	Normal Light Back Hen
Head and neck	Silvery grey	Silvery grey
Back and wings	Silvery grey	Silvery grey
Throat and breast	Silvery grey with black zebra stripes and breast bar	Silvery grey
Underparts	White	White
Cheek patches	Pale orange	Silvery grey to match breast
Side flanks	Orange with white spots	Silvery grey to match breast
Tear marks	Black	Black
Tail	Black with white bars	Black with white bars

Undesirable Features
Brown shading on back and wings.
General body colour too dark, showing insufficient dilution.
General patchiness of colour.
Dilution of any characteristic black markings, such as breast barring, tail etc.

Feature	Fawn Light Back Cock	Fawn Light Back Hen
Head and neck	Cream or pale fawn	Cream or pale fawn
Back and wings	Cream or pale fawn	Cream or pale fawn
Throat and breast	Cream or pale fawn with black zebra stripes and breast bar	Cream or pale fawn
Underparts	White	White or pale cream
Cheek patches	Pale orange	Cream or pale fawn to match breast
Side flanks	Orange with white spots	Cream or pale fawn to match breast
Tear marks	Black	Black
Tail	Black with white bars	Black with white bars

Undesirable Features
General body colour too dark, showing insufficient dilution.
General patchiness of colour.
Dilution of any characteristic black markings, such as breast barring, tail etc.

Of the colours currently recognised by the Zebra Finch Society, Light Backs are the most recent addition to the list of standard colours. Although only a colour standard for the Normal form of the mutation has been drawn up at present, it is possible to produce a Light Back form of all the other recognised colours, with the exception of Chestnut Flanked White. In my opinion it is correct to regard Light Backs as a form of Sex Linked Dilute, and at present they are exhibited in the Dilute or Silver classes, depending on the classification.

Visually they differ from the other forms of Dilute in that the black colour pigment retains its intensity, while other colour pigments are diluted. In fact, they appear to be the exact opposite of Recessive Dilutes. This mutation, although established for many years on the European Continent, only appeared in Britain during the late 1970s and since that time it has shown remarkable progress with regard to improvements in type and size. Generally, Light Backs have quite a long way to go before they catch up with colours such as Normals and Fawns, but if present progress is maintained, they could become regular contenders for major specials on the show bench.

Genetically, they are a sex-linked mutation, but various complications arise due to the mutation being very closely allied to Chestnut Flanked Whites. Apparently, the mutant gene responsible for both the Light Back and C.F.W. mutations occurs in exactly the same place on the X chromosome. This means that when the two different mutations are intermated, instead of some Normal-coloured young being produced, as would be expected, only Light Backs or C.F.W.s are bred. The close relationship between the two colours has led to Light Backs and C.F.W.s being regularly intermated, in the first place to build up stocks of Light Backs quickly, and in the second place to produce Light Backs of a paler body colour. While the use of Light Back x C.F.W. matings has produced lighter-coloured cock birds, it is generally true to say that Light Back hens do not show a lightening of colour. This is probably due to the fact that most of the Light Back cocks to show paler colour are Light Back/C.F.W. cocks, and as it is impossible to breed Light Back/C.F.W. hens, the hens will tend to be of a darker colour.

When mated to Normals, Light Backs behave in exactly the same genetic manner as other sex-linked mutations. When mated to C.F.W.s, it depends on the sex of the colours used and also whether the Light Back cocks are split for C.F.W. The vast majority of Light Back cocks are split for C.F.W., and when a bird of this type is mated to a C.F.W. hen, it is possible to produce Light Back/C.F.W. cocks, C.F.W. cocks, Light Back hens and C.F.W. hens. Should a genetically pure Light Back cock be mated to a C.F.W. hen, all the young will be visual Light Backs, but any cock birds produced are split for C.F.W. When a C.F.W. cock is mated to a Light Back hen, this will produce Light Back/C.F.W. cocks and C.F.W. hens.

Although there is a problem in producing cocks and hens which match for colour, careful selection of breeding stock and the gradual elimination of C.F.W. from studs of Light Backs will no doubt produce cocks and hens of the same shade of colour. While such birds may be a little darker than desired, allowances cannot be made for pairs in which the colour shade of the cock and the hen vary noticeably. To do this would be to ignore the quality of hens benched on the show bench and would therefore be the first step towards exhibiting Zebra Finches singly. Such a move would be a drastic change for the fancy, and Zebra Finches benched singly never display themselves as well as those exhibited in pairs.

There is as yet no standard for the Fawn form of Light Back, but these mutations can be combined, and I expect examples of this combination eventually to become very popular exhibition birds. It may appear impossible to combine these two sex-linked mutations, to produce Fawn Light Backs, as, in order to do so, the mutant genes responsible would need to be located on the same X chromosome. However, because of an occurrence called crossing-over, where X chromosomes within developing embryos randomly split and then recombine, Fawn Light Backs can be produced.

The best way to set about breeding this colour combination would be to mate a Fawn cock to a Light Back hen, as this would eliminate the possibility of a Light Back which is split for C.F.W. being used. Such a mating will produce Normal cocks which are split for both Light Back and Fawn. If these birds are remated to a Light Back hen or a Fawn hen, a small percentage of the young produced should be Fawn Light Back hens. The exact theoretical percentage cannot be determined accurately as the crossing-over of X chromosomes is random and this must occur in order to produce Fawn Light Backs. Matings of this type will also produce a number of Normal cocks, some of which will be split for both Fawn and Light

Back, but others only split for one of the two mutations, and not both. The next step would be to mate a Fawn Light Back hen to a Normal cock which is known to be split for both Light Back and Fawn, say a bird produced from a Fawn x Light Back mating. These matings should produce about 20 per cent Fawn Light Back cocks and hens. Once a few individual Fawn Light Backs have been bred, the task of building up numbers should not be too difficult. Fawn Light Backs could be mated to either Fawns or Light Backs to produce birds which can usefully be used in establishing greater numbers of Fawn Light Backs.

Remember, hens cannot carry sex-linked mutations in hidden form, and, therefore, when either a Fawn hen or a Normal Light Back hen are produced from matings between Fawns and Light Backs, they will be no more useful in establishing Fawn Light Backs than pure bred Fawns or pure bred Light Backs. It is the cocks which are of interest, as, although these may appear visually to be Fawns or Light Backs, they may be split for the other sex-linked colour. When mated to Fawn Light Back hens, 50 per cent of their young will, in theory, be Fawn Light Back cocks or hens. Pairing Fawn Light Back to Fawn Light Back will produce 100 per cent Fawn Light Back youngsters. Once sufficient numbers of these birds are produced, I expect a written colour standard will be adopted, just as in the case of Dominant and Recessive Creams. It would seem most sensible at the present time to exhibit them in the Dilute class, or, where the Dilutes are split into Silver and Cream classes, in the Cream class.

Some very attractive birds have been produced by combining the Dominant Dilute and Light Back mutations and these are bound to become more popular in the future. Matings combining the Dominant Silver and Normal Light Back forms can be calculated by using the mating lists describing pairings between Dominant Silvers and Fawns, substituting Fawn with Light Back and regarding Dominant Creams as Dominant Silver Light Backs.

Although Light Backs have been with us for a relatively short period of time, I am sure they will continue to grow in popularity, both on the show bench and in mixed collections. One of their most pleasing features, when first seen in Britain, was the evenness of colour on their backs and wings. Unless breeders are careful and resist the excessive use of too many buff-feathered birds, there is every chance that Light Backs will tend to become uneven and patchy-coloured, just as Dominant Dilutes did. They were also a very even shade of colour when first introduced, but the continual use of large coarse-feathered birds, in order to try to improve type and size, has spoilt many Dominant Dilutes. Let us hope breeders are prepared to be patient and build up quality gradually, rather than trying to achieve instant success.

Chestnut Flanked Whites

Feature	Chestnut Flanked White Cock	Chestnut Flanked White Hen
Head and neck	As near white as possible	As near white as possible, may have some darker head markings
Back and wings	As near white as possible	As near white as possible
Throat and breast	White with black or dark grey zebra stripes and breast bar	As near white as possible
Underparts	White	White
Cheek patches	Orange	White to match breast
Side flanks	Orange with white spots	White
Tear marks	Black or dark grey	Black or dark grey
Tail	White with black or grey bars	White with black or grey bars

Undesirable Features
Characteristic markings on cocks and hens too pale.
General body and wing colour not white enough.
Broken or poorly defined characteristic markings.
Hens showing too much dark feathering on head and neck.

Chestnut Flanked Whites are generally the second most popular mutation of Zebra Finch after Fawns, both in mixed collections and on the show bench. The basic concept of the colour form is a white-bodied bird which still retains its characteristic markings, these being tear marks, tail barring, breast barring, cheek patches and side flanks. Such an ideal is very attractive to many people and this, coupled with the fact

A Chestnut Flanked White cock and a Chestnut Flanked White hen, typical examples of the mutation as maintained by the majority of Zebra Finch breeders in Britain

that, genetically, it is a sex-linked mutation, has been largely responsible for their popularity. Sex-linked mutations can usually be easily established from just one or two individual birds in a relatively short period of time.

When first produced, these birds were known as Marked Whites, a term which naturally led to some confusion, as Zebras of the White mutation which carry mantling are also referred to as marked Whites. In order to clarify the situation, the Zebra Finch Society adopted the name Chestnut Flanked White which, despite its failings, has become widely accepted. In Zebra Finch circles, when there is talk of 'Chestnuts', and 'Flanks', or we see C.F.W., C.N.F.W. or C.N.F. White written, it is assumed that reference is being made to Chestnut Flanked Whites. This can be very confusing for the beginner, as to hear a conversation concerning 'Chestnuts' immediately

brings to mind some form of dark Fawn. 'Chestnut' is, however, the most commonly used spoken abbreviation of Chestnut Flanked White and C.F.W. the most usual written abbreviation. It is unlikely that these terms will be changed, and it would be difficult to find a more accurate simple description of the mutation.

The commonest failing of C.F.W.s is a tendency for characteristic markings to be washed out and lack good definition. At the present time, virtually all specialist C.F.W. breeders are aiming to produce birds which have good markings: without this the mutation loses much of its appeal. Ideally, in the fullness of time, it will be possible to breed C.F.W.s which have the same depth of colour and markings as Normal Zebras, coupled with a clean white general body colour. There is, however, still a long way to go in order to achieve

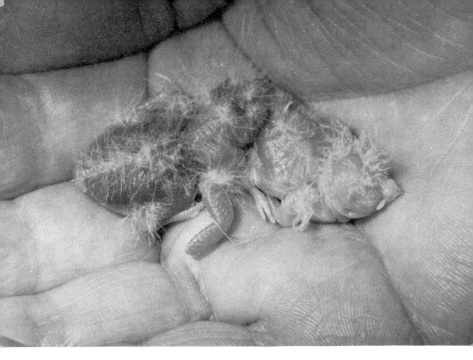

British C.F.W. and Continental C.F.W. chicks. The darker-skinned bird is charac-teristic of British birds, while the paler-skinned chick is a Continental C.F.W.

this ultimate goal, but great advances have been made over the past thirty years, and further improvements are bound to be realised in the years to come.

One particularly important feature is the cheek patch colour on cock birds, and most fanciers will agree that, without good colour in this area, C.F.W.s have little chance of success on the show bench. Over the years, by selective breeding, the cheek patch colour has gradually been improved and it is now accepted that these should be orange on good exhibition specimens. Prior to 1976, the Z.F.S. colour standard described C.F.W. cocks as having cream cheek patches; this was surpassed by many exhibition birds seen in the 1970s, and the standard was suitably ammended to orange. Despite this general improvement in cheek patch colour, it can be a difficult feature to establish in a stud of C.F.W.s and, without careful planning, is easily lost. One unusual feature I have noticed when breeding C.F.W.s, is that pairs which have produced good-coloured cocks during one season, when remated the following year, will often breed young cocks which are lacking in cheek patch colour. In fact, so few cock birds with good cheek patch colour have been bred from pairs consisting of two over-year birds, that I always use at least one young bird in every C.F.W. pairing made.

Tail barring is a feature commonly at fault on C.F.W.s, the dark tail bars usually being pale grey rather than dark grey or black. During the late 1970s, a number of C.F.W.s bred from Continental stock were seen by fanciers in Britain. Visually these differed quite considerably from most of the British C.F.W.s at that time. While the best examples of British birds displayed good cheek patch and side flank colour, nice clean white plumage, acceptable tear marks and breast barring, they did tend to lack good tail barring. The newly introduced birds, although tending to lack good cheek patch colour and purity of whiteness generally, showed greatly improved black markings, their tail barrings being particularly prominent. Not unnaturally, several breeders thought it would be worthwhile to try to combine the desirable features of the two styles of C.F.W. and so produce birds which more closely matched the ideal colour standard. This idea was fine in theory, and fanciers set about mating the two types of C.F.W. together, but, surprisingly, although very similar, they proved to be two different mutations.

The birds bred in Britain at that time were all dark-skinned when born, but when the Continental stock was used, a number of pink-skinned youngsters were produced. At first it was thought Whites had somehow been bred, as they have pink skins when chicks. This was not the case; the pink-skinned young turned out to be C.F.W.s of the Continental type. Initially, all the pink-skinned birds bred were hens and they also had quite pink eyes in the nest. Among the dark-skinned youngsters produced were some nicely marked cock birds which showed the desired improvement in tail markings, while still retaining the desirable features associated with British stock. These turned out to be birds which carried mutant genes for both of the different mutations and were generally regarded as being British C.F.W.s split for Continental C.F.W. In order to produce matched pairs, it was only necessary to produce some British C.F.W. split Continental C.F.W. hens. Unfortunately, because C.F.W. is a sex-linked mutation, this is impossible to achieve. Hens either have to be British C.F.W.s or Continental C.F.W.s; they cannot carry mutant genes for both mutations. Therefore, the hens produced either had good purity of general body colour, but lacked the desired darker tail barrings, or they possessed the good tail markings and were of a silvery grey general body colour. Once this fact was realised, many fanciers decided to concentrate on pure British C.F.W. stock which, apart from the tail barrings, tended to show more of the desired colour features and better type (shape) and size. A few fanciers continued breeding from Continental stock and these birds are seen occasionally.

With regard to exhibition, both types of C.F.W. are shown in the same class and both must be bred to the same standard. It was thought that a separate standard should be drawn up for the Continental C.F.W.s to make allowances for their silvery grey body colour. However, had this been done, it would also have been necessary to redraw the standard for British C.F.W.s, making allowances for the paler tail barrings. This would have led to a situation where two standards existed, neither of which described the 'ideal C.F.W.'. Therefore, anyone who did manage to produce that elusive ideal would find their birds were faulted by both standards. When exhibiting C.F.W.s, it is necessary to bench either a pair of British C.F.W.s or a pair of Continental C.F.W.s: the two mutations cannot be mixed to form one pair. The well-marked cock birds, regarded as British C.F.W.s split for Continental C.F.W., in theory cannot be exhibited as it is impossible to produce a matched partner. On occasions, it may be possible to show them with a good British C.F.W. and do well, but there is always the chance that a judge will decide two different mutations have been exhibited as a pair and penalise or even disqualify the exhibit.

The use of Normals is often advocated to improve the colour and markings in C.F.W.s, but unless one starts with a good-coloured C.F.W., or a bird bred from good-coloured C.F.W.s, it is very difficult to reproduce this feature in young birds. Virtually all the best-coloured C.F.W. cocks I have bred were produced from C.F.W. x C.F.W. matings, and I have yet to be convinced that using Normals improves colour. It can, however, improve both type and size, providing quality

The cock in this pair of Chestnut Flanked Whites is a product of intermating British and Continental stock and was bred by Barry Debling. It shows the darker tail barring characteristic of Continental stock. The hen is a pure bred British type C.F.W.

Normals are used, and therefore matings between both Normal cocks and C.F.W. hens, or C.F.W. cocks and Normal hens are recommended by leading breeders. Normal cock x C.F.W. hen matings will produce Normal/C.F.W. cocks and Normal hens, the Normal/C.F.W. cocks then being remated to C.F.W. hens to produce C.F.W. cocks and hens, Normal/C.F.W. cocks and Normal hens. C.F.W. cock x Normal hen matings will produce Normal/C.F.W. cocks and C.F.W. hens, both of which can be used to mate back to C.F.W.s.

Personally, I prefer to pair C.F.W. cocks to Normal hens when introducing Normals into C.F.W.s, this being done to try to breed C.F.W. hens of good type and size. These can then be mated back to good-coloured C.F.W. cocks, in the hope of producing birds with both good markings and good type. By using a C.F.W. cock in the initial mating, the visual colour of the bird used is a known factor. When a C.F.W. hen is used for mating to Normals, many of the visual colour characteristics are not known. As hens do not show cheek patches or side

117

flanks, the only possible way of determining the colour she is likely to pass on to her young, is by assessing her close male relatives. However, pairs of C.F.W.s often produce both good-coloured and poorly coloured cocks in the same nest and therefore hens which carry good colour and those which do not can both be bred from one pair. This means the colour qualities an untried hen can pass on to her offspring are never guaranteed. In order to produce C.F.W. cocks, her Normal/C.F.W. sons must be mated to another C.F.W. hen whose colour qualities are again assumed, rather than known. When the cocks appear, quite often their cheek patch colour is too diluted and two years' work has been for nothing. A number of breeders have out-crossed C.F.W.s to Fawns and this may well produce useful birds, especially hens. This is not a mating I personally favour, as the introduction of Fawn often produces birds of a creamy body colour, which is undesirable.

It is important to try to produce C.F.W.s which are of as pure a white in general coloration as possible, without losing definition in the markings. While the general impression given by good C.F.W.s is of a basically white bird, the plumage is never pure white, as displayed by good examples of the White mutation. In C.F.W.s, there is always a slight grey or fawn suffusion to the 'white' feathering. This may only be visible on close inspection, but it is present in virtually all examples of the mutation. To fault C.F.W.s for not being absolutely pure white would be wrong, but, at the same time, it is expected that good show birds should be reasonably 'white'. Hens are, in theory, permitted to carry some dark markings on the head and neck, but exhibitors and judges alike tend to look for birds which do not show these markings.

On occasions it is advocated that two distinct 'lines' of C.F.W.s should be maintained, one to breed good-coloured cocks and the other to produce clean white hens. Personally, I have not found this to be the case and have benched many winning pairs of C.F.W.s which consisted of a cock and hen bred from the same parents. At the same time, it is always worth retaining some of the darker hens produced for stock purposes, especially when they are related to good-coloured cocks. Such hens can often improve the characteristic markings in a stud of C.F.W.s, and, providing they are not over-used, will not have an adverse affect on the purity of white feathering displayed by their youngsters. Some time ago, in an attempt to breed hens which showed lighter head markings, C.F.W.s were mated to Dominant Dilutes. This was not a very good idea as, although head markings were reduced, the tear markings were also diluted and these should be shown prominently. As a form of Dilute C.F.W. can be produced, introducing a bird of this type into a stud of C.F.W.s could have disastrous consequences with regard to breeding well-marked C.F.W. cocks.

Specialist breeders of C.F.W.s would be well advised to pay particular attention to the feather types displayed by their birds. A policy of pairing buff to buff in order to produce better type C.F.W.s will soon result in pale-coloured specimens being bred. Mating yellow to yellow to improve colour will generally produce birds of poorer type. Where possible, buff-feathered birds should be mated to yellow-feathered

A nest of C.F.W. (British) Zebra Finches at about seventeen days of age. The darker-headed youngsters will generally turn out to be hens, while the cocks tend to be lighter-headed

birds with the aim of producing either yellows of good type or buffs which display good colour. In order to be successful with C.F.W.s at the highest level, usually one or other of these two ideals must be produced.

While this may be difficult to achieve, C.F.W.s have often featured as major specials' winners. The mutation started to vie regularly for top honours in the late 1960s, but their progress was halted slightly during the early 1970s with the dramatic upsurge in Whites. By the middle of the 1970s, C.F.W.s were often winning top honours at the highest levels of competition and continued to do so during the latter part of the 1970s. Their success faded slightly in the 1980s, but some excellent examples were still to be seen on the show bench and they still won a share of leading awards. At the present time, C.F.W.s have perhaps 'slipped from grace' somewhat, but the potential is still there for top quality pairs to be produced.

Penguins

Feature	Penguin Cock	Penguin Hen
Head and neck	Paler than usual shade shown by non-Penguin colour forms	Paler than usual shade shown by non-Penguin colour forms
Back and wings	Shade to match head and neck with lighter lacings on flights	Shade to match head and neck with lighter lacings on flights
	The lacing effect on the flights becomes more pronounced with successive moults	
Throat and breast	White with no trace of zebra stripes or breast bar	White
Underparts	White	White
Cheek patches	Orange	White
Side flanks	Reddish-orange with white spots	White
Tear marks	None	None
Tail	To match general body colour with white bars	To match general body colour with white bars

Undesirable Features
Traces of zebra throat stripes and breast barring on cocks.

The Penguin variety differs in a number of ways from other colour forms, but the most striking difference is the absence of throat markings and breast barring on cock birds. This white-fronted appearance is responsible for the use of the term 'Penguin' to describe the mutation. Other colour variations also include the absence of tear marks, dilution of tail barring and a lacing effect on the wings. Hens, in addition to the previously mentioned features, also show white cheek patches. At one time there was a Penguin mutation which was quite dark on the wings and back, and such a bird would be more penguin-like than the birds currently seen. This variety has largely died out, partly due to the wording of the Zebra Finch Society colour standard which specifically requested Penguins to show lacing on the wings. As exhibition birds, the darker-backed specimens were immediately faulted and lost favour with most Penguin specialists. Even the lighter form of Penguin lacks popularity with the exhibition fancy, probably because the mutation is associated with poor type and size.

It is possible to breed various different colour forms of Penguin Zebras, but Normal and Fawn Penguins are generally the most effective visually. Over the years, a number of different fanciers have tried to establish good exhibition strains of Penguin Zebras, but there is always a tendency for these birds to lack the cobby type essential these days for any form of exhibition Zebras, and, consequently, they rarely enjoy much success. An occasional pair have taken leading awards at major shows, but it has proved extremely difficult to maintain quality and type in future generations. Some very good non-Penguin birds have been utilised in order to try to establish good type in Penguin stock. This has inevitably spoilt the quality of the non-Penguin birds produced, rather than effecting any permanent improvement in the Penguins.

To improve the type and size would undoubtedly take years of intermating with good quality Normals or Fawns. Not only do very few breeders have adequate stocks of non-Penguin birds available, these matings often result in traces of breast barring being shown by the Penguin cocks produced. As the clear chest is an essential characteristic of the mutation, birds with such faults cannot be expected to win major awards on the show bench, no matter what other virtues they may possess. Fawn hens which lack tear marks are produced quite regularly by breeders of Fawns, and these birds could be useful out-crosses for breeders of Penguins. Fanciers who breed mismarked Fawns of this type should perhaps consider offering them to Penguin specialists, rather than selling them as pet birds.

In addition to the inherent type and breast marking faults, problems can also be caused by the wing lacings. Not only does it take a number of moults for this marking pattern to be fully established, but cock Penguins tend to display the lacing effect more quickly than hens. This means it can be difficult to exhibit matched pairs of current-year bred birds, as young cocks and young hens will be at different stages of developing their lacings at any given time during the show season. The 'ideal' Penguin would indeed be a very attractive bird, but, unfortunately, I have seen very few birds which even approached this ideal during the past twenty years.

Genetically, Penguin is a recessive mutation and inherited in a similar fashion to other recessive colour forms, such as Pied. With Pieds, birds tend to maintain their quality when produced from Pied x Pied matings, but Penguins from Penguin x Penguin pairings generally do not. Because of this there was speculation in the past that they were, in fact, a miniature variety, but this theory is now generally discounted. To maintain quality, it is usually necessary to use Penguin x Normal or Penguin x Fawn matings, which results in either Normal/Penguins or Fawn/Penguins being bred. Should two split Penguins be mated together, in theory, 25 per cent of the young produced are Penguins, 50 per cent are split Penguin and 25 per cent will not carry any genes for the Penguin mutation at all. If a visual Penguin and a split Penguin are mated together, the young produced will either be Penguins or split Penguins. The most useful matings are therefore Penguin x Penguin, non-Penguin x Penguin and Penguin x split Penguin, as all these give birds of known genetical make-up.

Although split Penguin x split Penguin matings have the drawback of producing birds whose genetic make-up would be unknown without the aid of test matings, some years ago my father bred some Penguins quite unexpectedly from a pair of visual Normals. The young turned out to be quite good examples of the Penguin mutation, with reasonably good markings and better type and size than is usually associated with Penguins. The birds were given to a specialist Penguin breeder, as we did not have the facilities to add another colour to our stud of birds. On reflection, I think the best course of action with these birds would have been to mate them to Normals and produce more splits, these could then have been intermated to produce Penguins without introducing any Penguins from another source. The introduction of other Penguins would, in the fullness of time, reproduce the poor type and size characteristics of these birds and any short term improvement would eventually have been lost. While the markings may have suffered initially by matings to non-Penguin birds, this could be given more attention in later years, once examples of the breed, which showed better type and size, had been established.

It is a pity more Penguins are not seen on the show bench, but for any bird to become popular, it must be attractive to a wide range of fanciers, so that large numbers are being bred annually. Penguins have little chance of achieving this status at the present time, and therefore large improvements are unlikely to be realised in the foreseeable future. There have been various suggestions that a number of established fanciers should start to keep studs of Penguins to prevent the breed dying out. However, it is impossible to force any individual to

A Normal Penguin cock. This bird was bred from a pair of visual Normals. In order to produce Penguin youngsters both parents must have been 'split' for Penguin

keep birds of a particular mutation and very few breeders have the facilities to add an extra colour to their existing studs.

Yellow-Beaks

Feature	Yellow-Beak Cock	Yellow-Beak Hen
All features except beak, feet and legs	As red-beaked form of same colour or mutation	As red-beaked form of same colour or mutation
Beak, feet and legs	Yellow or orange	Yellow or orange

Undesirable Features
Insufficient dilution of beak colour.
Particular faults as detailed for appropriate red-beaked forms.

During the late 1960s and early 1970s, a number of breeders produced a few Yellow-Beaked (for want of a better name) Zebra Finches. The majority of these birds actually appeared to have orangey-coloured beaks and looked like red-beaked birds which were off colour. Yellow-Beaks were, however, recognised as a distinct mutation and accepted as a standard colour by the Zebra Finch Society. Genetically, the mutation is recessive and may be produced unexpectedly, from time to time, from pairs of red-beaked birds.

When first accepted into the standards, they were shown in the Penguin and A.O.C. class, much to the annoyance of specialist Penguin breeders. The situation has now been ammended and pairs of Yellow-Beaks are exhibited in the same class as they would normally be shown in if they were red-beaked birds, i.e. Fawn Yellow-Beaks are exhibited in the Fawn class, Pied Yellow-Beaks in the Pied class, etc. The mutation has found very little favour among specialist Zebra Finch breeders, but occasionally pairs are on the show bench and they have won specials from time to time.

Perhaps the only colour form which may possibly benefit aesthetically by having yellow beaks are Dilutes, as it could be argued that the diluted beak colour matches the dilution of the birds. The best examples of Yellow-Beaks I have seen were Pied Whites, and these had definite yellow-coloured beaks and could not be mistaken for red-beaked birds. Generally, I find Yellow-Beaks have very little to recommend them, in their own right, and I much prefer Zebra Finches with red beaks.

Non-Standard Varieties

There are a number of Zebra Finch mutations being bred throughout the world which, at the present time, are not recognised with regard to exhibition by the Zebra Finch Society. The main reason for these new varieties not being recognised is simply a lack of substantiated information about them. Once breeders have produced examples of new mutations for themselves, ascertained' their method of genetic inheritance and can differentiate between good and bad specimens, with regard to colour, there is every likelihood that these mutations will be accepted as standard colours.

Unfortunately, the Z.F.S. does not have any set guide lines as to what requirements must be met by a new mutation before it can become recognised. However, various conditions could be adopted to safeguard the colours which presently form the 'backbone' of the exhibition fancy. These conditions should be designed to prevent adopting, as recognised colours, any mutations which are associated with congenital physical disorders, have been derived by hybridisation, or are not true breeding. Colour standards for new mutations cannot be drawn up correctly unless there is a consensus of opinion from several fanciers who have bred at least first- and second-generation examples of the new mutation in question. There is no point in adopting a new mutation as a recognised colour unless it has been shown that there is a genuine desire on the part of breeders to exhibit the mutation competitively. Providing classes for birds which nobody wishes to exhibit is senseless and all fancies must guard against adopting large show classifications that destroy competition.

A policy of continually intermating closely related birds and retaining any which are unusually marked will often result in the production of new mutations. In Britain, close relatives are only mated together on a very limited scale and many serious breeders will, on producing anything slightly unusual, despatch it to the pet shop as being of no use for the production of exhibition quality birds. Consequently, very few new mutations come to light in Britain, but quite a number are bred in other countries, notably on the European Continent. It is impossible for me to give precise descriptions of these 'new' mutations as I have only seen a very limited number. Not until

One of the first pairs of Black Breasted Zebra Finches to be seen at a show in Britain. These birds were owned by Barry Debling and were seen at the 1977 M.Z.F.C. Club Show

many birds have been seen is it possible to say which features are desirable and which are not.

Albino
An Albino Zebra Finch should be the same in all respects as albino forms of other white-ground birds. That is to say, a bird of pure white plumage with pink eyes. Genetically it should be sex-linked.

Black Breasted
The Black Breasted mutation has a number of features which differ from the normal form. As the name suggests, it displays a broad breast bar, above which is a lighter bib, mottled with dark feathering. There are no zebra throat stripes, as displayed

by most of the recognised mutations. The cheek patches do not have definite boundaries, orange feathering spreads onto the head, neck and shoulders, with tear marks being absent. Side flanks seem to be poorly defined and are marked with white ticks rather than spots. The tail, although normally coloured, is not definitely barred as in most other forms, the alignment of dark and light feathers being somewhat haphazard. Black Breasted hens show traces of a breast bar. Genetically it is regarded as a recessive mutation, but birds split for Black Breasted can be identified visually and therefore this indicates incomplete dominance.

Orange Breasted
The Orange Breasted mutation mainly differs from the nor-

mal form in that various amounts of orange feathering are present on the breast and also in regions where other black markings occur. This effectively means that tear markings are absent, or at least partially masked by orange. Orange Breasted Normals do, however, still display some black zebra throat stripes and black tail bars. When combined with the Black Breasted mutation, birds which show quite considerable amounts of orange feathering on the head, neck, face, throat and breast are produced. These have very little of the clarity and precision of markings which British breeders repeatedly try to establish in their stocks. The mutation is regarded as being recessive genetically and can be combined with all other colour forms. It may well be generally more attractive when combined with mutations which are paler than Normals.

Phaeo

The Phaeo mutation is a rather more recently developed mutation than the Black Breasted form, although it would seem to be similar in some respects. The cheek patches spread onto the head, neck and shoulders, it has a light bib beneath the beak, and the tear marks appear to be absent. The general over-all colour is diluted or reduced to nearly white, except that back and wing feathers are edged with orange or deep fawn. This is a reversal of the lacing effect shown by Penguins where the feathers have light edges. The breast bar is more akin to that shown by some forms of Orange Breasted Zebras and the tail barrings are virtually absent.

Isabel

The Isabel mutation is reported to be a form of recessive dilute, although it does appear much lighter generally than those birds regarded as Recessive Dilutes by the Z.F.S. The over-all body colour is quite pale, being off-white on the back and wings. Black markings are very diluted, to the point where they are almost absent, but cheek patches and side flanks are displayed quite prominently.

Agate

The Agate mutation appears to be another form of dilute, not dissimilar to a poor Light Back visually. The Normal Agate could be described as a bird with the head colour of a Normal, but the body and wing colour of a light Fawn. Cheek patches, side flanks and black markings are all slightly diluted.

Grey Cheeked

The Grey Cheeked mutation would seem similar to the Normal, except that cheek patches are shaded with grey in both cocks and hens. It may well be that the mutation is best displayed by paler colour forms. Grey Cheeks may also be referred to as Lead Cheeked.

Fawn Cheeked

Fawn Cheeked Zebras appear little different to the Grey Cheeked mutation, except that the cheek patches on cocks and hens are shaded with Fawn.

Black Cheeked

The Black Cheeked mutation differs from the Normal in that the cheek patches and side flanks are black instead of being deep orange or chestnut. When transferred to lighter colour forms, the cheek patches and side flanks would seem to lose much of their intensity. This mutation is believed to be dominant genetically.

Black Faced

Black Faced Zebras have very dark breasts, with black markings spreading onto the underparts. The small triangular shape between the beak and tear mark is black and the cheek patches and side flanks are brown. They are very similar visually to those birds often described as being melanistic. Melanistic birds, however, only retain their darker feathering until the second moult when they take on the appearance of Normal Zebras. This is caused by a liver deficiency when the birds are very young, which is corrected in later life. No doubt the Black Faced mutation is not a temporary condition and remains with the bird for life.

Crested

These should appear like uncrested forms in all respects, except for displaying a head crest. The most desirable type of crest would be similar to that displayed by Gloster Corona

An example of a Crested Normal Zebra Finch, seen at the 1977 M.Z.F.C. Club Show and owned by Barry Debling

Canaries, but all examples of the breed I have seen are a long way from that ideal. It has been suggested that Crests should be exhibited as one Crest and one non-crest. Personally I would oppose this point of view, as there is a great danger on the show bench, as the crests displayed are so poor generally, that judges would resort to placing the pair containing the best non-crest, first in the class.

Florida Zebras
The Florida Zebra mutation has been developed in the United States of America and appears visually to be very similar to a Chestnut Flanked White Penguin Zebra Finch. I assume it is not simply a combination of these two mutations, as this would mean it was no more a new mutation than Fawn Penguins, for example.

No mutation can become well established unless it is attractive to many different breeders. Those breeders who wish to have non-standard varieties recognised must be prepared to exhibit them in the Non-Standard Variety class as frequently as possible. They must also stimulate extra interest by making their breeding results known to the fancy in general and so encourage others to specialise in the breeds.

8 Exhibition Standards

When one species of bird is regularly bred in captivity it is inevitable that birdkeepers will want to compare their stock with birds bred by other enthusiasts. The only realistic method of doing this is by means of competitive exhibition. If all the birds are staged in similar cages and judged to the same standards, then one can assess which are the best on display. Although various prizes are offered at shows, the main benefit to exhibitors, win or lose, is being able to compare birds from different studs. Additionally, the exhibition fancy enables people to meet new friends, from all parts of the country, who share a common interest.

When only a few birds of one species are being exhibited, they can usually be assessed on condition and presentation alone. However, when any bird becomes very popular on the show bench, it is necessary to adopt exhibition standards for type (shape) , colour and markings, in addition to those for condition. This is the situation within the Zebra Finch Fancy where, due to the popularity of these birds, it has been necessary to draw up detailed exhibition standards. Generally, standards originate from a consensus of opinion from within the fancy and may be modified slightly as the fancy progresses. In Britain the majority of Zebra Finches are exhibited in true pairs of the same colour or mutation and judged to the Zebra Finch Society exhibition standards which are as follows:

CONDITION to be essential. Birds should not receive any award unless they are in show condition. Missing, ragged or soiled feathers, and missing claws or toes constitute show faults.
TYPE Bold throughout and of 'Cobby' type, giving the birds a look of substance; wings evenly carried to root of tail.
MARKINGS (Where applicable) COCKS – Chest bar distinct and

clear cut, not less than ¹/₈ in. (3mm.) deep and of even depth throughout. Throat evenly striped. Side flankings should be prominent extending from the wing butts to the end of the rump and decorated with round, clearly defined white spots. Cheek patches and tear markings to be clear and distinct. Beak bright red with feet and legs deep pink.

HENS – as for Cocks, less chest bar, throat markings, side flank markings and cheek patches. Beaks a paler shade of red. Cock markings on hens are definite show faults.

The birds as a pair should have a balanced appearance.

In addition to the basic show standards, there are also colour standards. These apply to each specific recognised colour of Zebra Finch and should be studied by anyone interested in exhibiting their birds. New colours, for which no standard exists, cannot be entered in direct competition against the recognised colours, for, without a standard, there is no way of judging whether they are good or bad examples of that mutation. Classes are, however, provided for non-standard colours, so that fanciers may have an opportunity to view these birds. If any new colours are attractive to a wide cross-section of the hobby, they soon became popular, a colour standard is drawn up and they are recognised for exhibition purposes.

Exhibition standards are sometimes charged with being artificial and therefore unethical. Provided fit healthy birds, with no congenital physical disorders are being produced, the breeding of exhibition stock can only serve to enhance our practical knowledge of that species of bird. The first essential of producing type standard show birds is to breed birds to a given standard, and should the need ever arise to breed birds to a different standard, say for reintroduction into the wild, the skill and expertise gained by fanciers attempting to produce exhibition birds will be invaluable. Anyone with the ability to produce birds to one standard should, given a little time, be able to produce birds to any other standard required. Additionally, in the process of breeding exhibition birds, it is necessary to successfully mate together two specific individual birds, which is much more difficult than breeding from birds in a random fashion where they are allowed to select their own mates. Come the day when aviculturists are allowed to make their contribution in preventing the extinction of endangered species, by captive breeding, the need will be to breed from specific individual birds and not a large mixed collection. While the breeding of Zebra Finches may seem a long way removed from that of endangered species, the knowledge gained by breeding from hundreds of pairs, over tens of years, encountering virtually every conceivable problem, can be very useful to anyone attempting to breed from a very limited stock of birds.

Show Cages

Whenever possible, Z.F.S. standard show cages should be used to exhibit Zebra Finches. The specification for the Z.F.S. standard show cage is as follows:

A standard Z.F.S. show cage

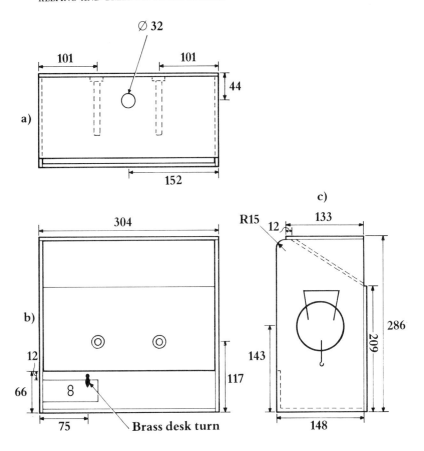

Plans of Z.F.S. Standard Show Cage: a) Plan; b) Front view; c) End view; d) Wire front; e) Drinker door; f) S hook; g) Desk turn; h) Door
All measurements shown in millimetres.

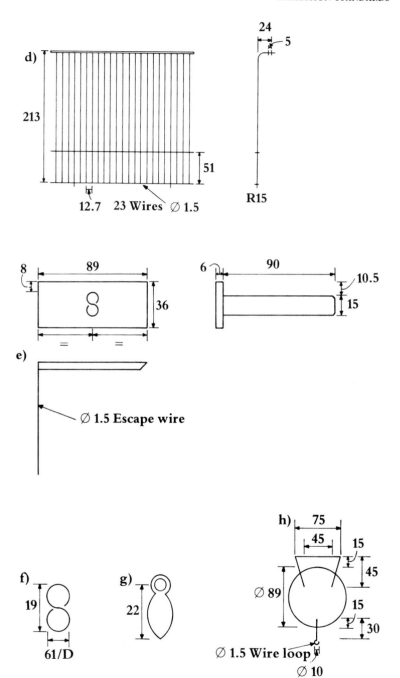

d) 213

51

12.7 23 Wires ⌀ 1.5

24

5

R15

8 89

36

= =

6 90

10.5

15

e)

⌀ 1.5 Escape wire

f) 19

61/D

g) 22

h) 75

45

15

45

15

30

⌀ 89

⌀ 1.5 Wire loop

⌀ 10

Specification

Wood:
Top, Sides, Bottom, False Roof and Front Rail 6mm thick. Back 4mm thick ply. [Front rail may be 9mm thick if preferred.]

Perches:
Over-all length, 100mm. 10mm. Dia. Rear boss, 25mm. Dia. projecting, 10mm.

Front Rail:
Right hand edge of the drinker door cut at 45 degrees. Escape wire (painted white) fitted into other end. 'S' hook fastened to the centre of the drinker door with a staple as shown. Drinker door fastened by a brass desk turn painted black. Door hinged using pin through front rail and door. Zinc clip screwed to the inside of door to carry white plastic drinker.

Wire Front:
Comprising 23 wires 127mm centre to centre, double punched bar at top set 5mm apart, for fixing two wires left top and bottom.

Colour:
Inside white. Outside black.

Floor Covering:
Any suitable seed.

Birds not exhibited in standard cages are ineligible to receive awards offered by specialist Zebra Finch clubs. However, they are not automatically disqualified and may be eligible to win class awards and specials offered by local cage bird societies. Naturally, it would be disappointing to find birds have done well at a show, only to be debarred from winning several awards because they were in the wrong type of cage.

The use of standard cages is important for two main reasons. Firstly, it provides a uniform setting for the birds, making comparions between exhibits easier, and secondly, it prevents the use of unique show cages which could indicate to judges the ownership of exhibits.

On occasions, bird shows are criticised for the size of cages used to display birds. The design of these cages is based on years of practical experience. They display the birds well and can be handled easily by show officials. Additionally, they are ideally suited for transporting birds and offer them familiar surroundings despite being outside their own birdroom. The birds staged at shows are not kept in show cages throughout their lives, only for the duration of shows. On being returned to their own birdroom, they probably enjoy far better care and management than many birds kept purely for breeding purposes.

Exhibition Status

In order to give new exhibitors a fair chance of winning awards, the exhibition of Zebra Finches is split into two main sections, one for champions and the other for novices. All beginners should show as novices, as once birds are entered in the champion section, exhibitors cannot revert to being novices. The period spent in the novice section allows fanciers to learn the art of preparing birds for exhibition without having to compete directly against very experienced fanciers. Although a number of awards have to be won before promotion to champion status, the term champion refers more to the experience gained within the exhibition fancy, than it does to the quality of birds maintained. Because an exhibitor is a champion, it does not mean the birds maintained are of a particular standard. Naturally, most champions will keep a stud of good quality birds, but this need not always be the case. Any exhibitor can become a champion simply by electing to exhibit their birds in the champion classes. In addition to the champion and novice sections, junior classes also exist within the Zebra Finch section, for the sake of young fanciers interested in exhibiting their birds.

Show Classifications

The most commonly seen show classification for Zebras at Zebra Finch Society patronage shows offers a total of nineteen classes. These are as follows:

CHAMPION	NOVICE
Normal	Normal
Fawn	Fawn
Pied	Pied
Dilute (inc. Light Back)	Dilute (inc. Light Back)
Chestnut Flanked White	Chestnut Flanked White
White	White
Penguin	Penguin
Non Standard Variety	Non Standard Variety

JUNIOR
Normal
Fawn
Any Other Colour

All the classes are for true pairs of the same colour. The Normal, Fawn, Chestnut Flanked White and White classes are for birds of these colours which are not visual Pieds, Penguins or Dilutes. All Pieds are exhibited in the Pied class, but must still be pairs of the same colour. All Penguins, except Penguin Pieds, are shown in the Penguin class in pairs of the same colour. Normal and Fawn Dilutes, except any which are also Pied or Penguin, are shown in the Dilute class, including pairs of Dominant or Recessive Silvers, Dominant or Recessive Creams and Light Backs. Yellow-Beaked forms are shown in the class they would be exhibited in if they were red-beaked. The junior Any Other Colour class is for all recognised forms of Zebra Finch, excluding Normals and Fawns. Mutations not as yet recognised by the Z.F.S. are shown in the Non-Standard Variety class.

At a number of shows, referred to as club shows, larger classifications are provided. These split Dilutes into two classes, one for Silvers and Normal Light Backs, and the other for Creams. All the classes are then divided into two sections, one for adult birds and the other for breeder birds. Only birds rung with the current-year, closed, coded Z.F.S. rings of the exhibitor can be entered in breeder classes, but any birds, even young current-year bred birds, can be shown in adult classes. This classification is usually seen at shows catering solely for Zebra Finches, often staged by specialist Zebra Finch clubs.

In addition to exhibition standards, each section should draw up a set of show rules. The Z.F.S. Show Rules are as follows:

Zebra Finch Society Show Rules

1 Zebra Finches must be shown in true pairs of the same colour.

2 The colour feeding of Zebra Finches is debarred.

3 The trimming of wings and/or tail is debarred.

4 All pairs of birds entered as Breeders and nominated 'BBE' (Bred by exhibitor) must carry the closed, coded current year dated rings of the Breeder (purchased through the Zebra Finch Society) and be exhibited by that Breeder.

5 Zebra Finches wearing more than one closed coded ring will be disqualified at Patronage Shows (N.B. one celluloid split ring and one closed coded ring are acceptable.)

6 Official closed coded rings purchased through the Zebra Finch Society must not be cut or altered for the purpose of putting them on the leg of a Zebra Finch.

7 28th February shall be deemed to end the exhibition year. Thus a bird hatched at any time during the current year can compete as a Breeder up to 28th February in the following year.

8 Zebra Finches should be shown in Standard Show Cages, the floor covering being any seed suitable for Zebra Finches. Pairs not exhibited in standard show cages are not eligible to compete for Zebra Finch Society specials.

9 A Judge's decision is final except in the case of misrepresentation, intentional or otherwise.

10 Special Prizes offered by the Zebra Finch Society shall only be competed for at Patronage Shows. Members must mark their entry forms 'ZFS'. Failure to do so debars the exhibitor from taking any Zebra Finch Society awards.

11 Definition of Novice Status. A Novice may exhibit in Novice Classes for five show seasons or until he/she has seven full wins with Breeder Birds at Area Club Show Patronage or Full Patronage Shows, whichever is the longer period.

Wins can be obtained in the following ways:

(a) A first prize with Breeder Birds in a class of seven or more exhibits, benched by three or more exhibitors.

(b) A Breeders' Rosette will count as one win, except where the exhibit has already won a class of seven exhibits (the same rule applying, seven exhibits, three exhibitors in the Breeder Section).

A member deciding to exhibit in Champion Classes cannot revert to Novice Classes.

12 Definition of Junior Status. Junior members may exhibit in Junior Classes from the age of 6 up to and including the show season in which they attain the age of 16. A Junior deciding to exhibit in Novice Classes cannot revert to Junior Classes.

13 Where two or more exhibitors keep or breed their Zebra Finches at one establishment, aviary or dwelling, such exhibitors must exhibit in the highest status of the said exhibitors (N.B. this rule does not apply to Junior Members).

14 Method of awarding points. In each class points are awarded for the first seven, i.e. 7 – 1st, 6 – 2nd, etc., unless there is less than seven when amount of birds actually Benched to count i.e. class of three – 3, 2, 1. If an entry in a small class wins Breeder or Adult Rosette bonus points are added to bring it up to 7. Individual colours are added together for Adult points and 'BBE' nominations for Breeders' points.

15 Any matters not mentioned in these rules will be dealt with by the Zebra Finch Society Committee, whose decision is final.

(Rule 14 refers to the method of awarding points for the purpose of ZFS points trophies.)

Entering Exhibits

In order to enter birds at a show, it is necessary to obtain a show schedule from the show secretary of the promoting club. The show schedule usually contains several hundred classes for various different types of birds, and also lists patronages granted to the show by specialist societies. Enclosed with the schedule will be an entry form, to be completed by anyone wishing to exhibit at the show. After filling in the entry form, it is advisable to make a copy which may be referred to if required. If there is any doubt as to how the entry form should be completed, a more experienced local fancier may be able to help. When the entry form has been completed and signed, it should be sent to the show secretary, together with a stamped self-addressed envelope, the required entry fees and any membership fees necessary. Always try to ensure that entries are made out properly. At worst mistakes can cost the exhibitor prizes, at best they make a lot of extra work for the show officials. A typical completed entry form may appear as follows:

CLASS NO	SECS. USE ONLY	DESCRIPTION OF EXHIBIT	NOMINATIONS	SELLING PRICE
276		Breeder Fawn Zebras	ZFS, BBE	NFS
277		Adult Pied Zebras	ZFS	NFS
277		Breeder Pied Zebras	ZFS, BBE	NFS
280		Adult White Zebras	ZFS	£7–00

The initials NFS in the selling price column are used to indicate that birds entered are not for sale, BBE is the accepted abbreviation for birds entered as breeders. Other details to look for in the show schedule are the times when birds can be benched before judging takes place, the time the show opens to the public and the time birds may be lifted or removed from the show. A few days before the show, cage labels will be received, and some events also issue lifting cards which should be kept safe and taken to the show so that exhibits can be claimed at lifting time.

A display of major special winners at one of the leading Zebra Finch shows

Competitive exhibition is the only way of assessing the true quality of birds. Additionally, it can also be both interesting and stimulating, adding a whole new perspective to the keeping and breeding of birds.

9 Exhibition Preparation

Once a birdkeeper has decided to try to attain the show standards, the keeping of birds takes on a whole new aspect. It is no longer sufficient simply to keep and breed birds; a new goal has been realised, and attempting to reach that goal can be a most challenging and satisfying experience. The initial requirement is to try to breed birds which will conform to the show standards, and then these birds must be correctly exhibited in order to meet with any degree of success.

The first part of the exhibition standard stresses the importance of condition with regard to show birds. This idea is the prime requirement of all exhibition birds. No one should ever expect to win prizes with birds which are poorly turned out. Zebra Finches are far more difficult to get into good show condition than one might at first imagine.

Being non-seasonal birds they can, and do, moult at any time of year, and they may moult more than once in any twelve-month period. Seasonal birds, such as Canaries, usually only moult once a year, and this having been successfully completed, they will not moult again until the following year. This is a great advantage when exhibiting birds as, providing the birds are not overshown, the whole show team will be available for exhibition at any given event. With Zebra Finches, one is never certain of being able to bench specific birds at any particular event. Birds which are in good condition and have moulted once, may suddenly go into another moult without warning. The problem is further compounded when Zebra Finches are exhibited in pairs. On occasions it may be that several cock birds are in condition, but no hens are ready, or vice versa, making it impossible to bench even one pair in good condition. Nevertheless, the non-seasonal nature of Zebra Finches does extend the show season, with some events being as early as June and others being held in December or even January. This means that, at some point during the show season, you should be able to bench well-matched pairs in good condition.

Unfortunately Zebra Finches also have a bad habit of squabbling and feather plucking when housed in the company of other Zebras. This means that to have a realistic chance of benching birds which are feather perfect, they will have to be housed in separate cages. Sometimes two hens will enjoy each other's company and occupy the same cage without any problems, but the only method of finding out which hens will be kindly disposed to one another is by trial and error. Cock birds, on the other hand, will usually squabble amongst themselves and the best potential show birds really need to be kept in a cage on their own. Isolation will not be in any way detrimental to the well being of the birds so long as they can hear other Zebra Finches in the same birdroom. One particularly annoying habit with relation to feather plucking, is when a bird continually pulls the tail barrings out of its exhibition partner. If the birds are kept separated until just before the show, and judged early in the day, the pair may be placed in accordance to their appearance with complete tails. More often than not, by the time judging takes place, the damage has been done and, realistically, it is a waste of time exhibiting birds which are going to spoil the appearance of their mate.

Selecting Show Birds

Exhibitors will usually select the basis of their show team about six weeks before the first show at which they intend to exhibit. This involves assessing all the available stock and selecting those with the best shape, colour and markings. As the birds are caught up, their feet should be checked to make sure they have no missing claws or toes. As stated in the standard, a missing claw or toe constitutes a show fault, and therefore birds with incomplete feet must be penalised by the judge. Outstanding birds with a missing claw may, on occasions, win a class, usually in poor competition, but they should never be awarded any major specials. At the same time as feet are being checked, the plumage can also be examined. Birds which have broken or ragged tail feathers should have these gently removed so that new feathers can regrow before the start of the show season. It will usually take Zebra Finches about six weeks to regrow a tail. Broken wing feathers can also be removed, but this is a much more delicate operation and should not be attempted unless you are confident of drawing the feather without damaging the wing.

Having selected the best possible birds and housed them in separate cages, or in twos if it is absolutely necessary, one can then begin to take stock of the birds available. If there are cocks or hens for which there is no available partner of the same colour, then these can be returned to the stock cages. It is pointless preparing a Silver cock bird for exhibition, even though he may be outstanding, if there is no Silver hen with which he can be exhibited. The markings displayed by the selected birds can also be closely examined at this time. Bad marking faults include the absence, on either cocks or hens, of any characteristic marking which the standard requires to be present. Equally undesirable are breast barring, ghost cheek patch markings or flank spots on hens, and faulted markings on cocks, such as broken breast bars or side flankings which

Zebra Finches must be in good condition to have any chance of being successful on the show bench. This Normal cock, although it has won at a number of shows, was not fully through the 'moult' when photographed and therefore appears 'rough'. It is not ready to be exhibited and would be most unlikely to gain any awards if benched

show no spots. Birds with any of these faults should be penalised on the show bench. On occasions, I have seen birds with marking faults quite highly placed at shows, perhaps due to a poor level of competition, or simply human error. This, of course, can be quite disconcerting to the beginner, but, as in all things where human judgement is involved, mistakes do occur from time to time. Over the years, by the law of averages, while one may feel hard done by on certain occasions, the balance will be redressed in the fullness of time and there will also be instances when your own birds are more highly placed than perhaps they deserve.

Pre-show Care

Once the preliminary checks are concluded, most birds will require quite intensive care so that they can be benched to their full potential. In order to promote good feather condition, the birds will need to be provided with baths as often as possible, and also sprayed regularly with lukewarm water. When spraying birds it is best to reserve a separate cage for this purpose, otherwise stock cages may become excessively damp. An ordinary pressure spray, as used by gardeners, is quite suitable for spraying birds, but do not use one which has previously contained weedkillers or other toxic chemicals. It is advisable to buy a brand new spray and use it exclusively for your birds. I use boiled water which has been allowed to cool until tepid for spraying birds, and many fanciers will also put various additives into the water, which are believed to improve feather condition. These include a drop of glycerine, a teaspoonful of bay rum, or even a drop of washing up liquid to each pint of water used, and there are also preparations commercially available, made specifically for birds, such as Plumespray. While these additives may well be beneficial, the actual spraying itself is the most important factor. Birds can be sprayed quite heavily leading up to the show season, but only require a light final spray before each show. Usually the final spray is given three days before being shown, and after this it may be advisable to prevent show birds bathing excessively until they return from being exhibited.

Hand-washing

Hand-washing potential exhibition birds may sometimes be

recommended by experienced fanciers. Personally I believe this is a vastly over-rated practice and should never be attempted by anyone inexperienced in the art. I have known many Zebras to be damaged, in one way or another, by hand-washing, while it has improved very few. The idea of hand-washing is not to get the bird clean, it is to remove some of the natural oils from the plumage of the birds and so enhance their apparent type and size. The removal of these oils makes birds very susceptible to cold and they should be housed indoors, at least overnight, after they have been washed. Birds are not washed prior to every show. The full benefit, if any, only becomes evident about two to three weeks after washing. As most Zebra Finches show distinct marking patterns, these can be temporarily damaged by hand-washing, making the process an entire waste of time. Washing is also advocated to remove the small wax-covered pin feathers on the heads and necks of birds, which can spoil their appearance. Pin feathers can be a problem, especially when birds are housed individually, but hand-washing is probably the most risky method of removing the wax coverings.

Birds kept in groups soon have the wax coverings removed by mutual preening between individuals and preening is the best way of solving the problem. Should birds be available which are neither required for exhibition nor partial to feather plucking, these can be used as 'grooms', simply by placing them in the company of the bird which is showing pin feathers. Of course, if faced with the choice between waiting a couple of weeks for the feathers to break naturally, or risking a bird being plucked and totally spoilt, it is much wiser to be patient. Where there are just a few pin feathers left to 'break', it may be possible to brush these out gently, a few days before the bird is due to be exhibited.

Show Training

Potential show birds will require show training before being exhibited. This allows them to become accustomed to their show cage and so perform confidently when placed before the judge. Birds which refuse to perch when staged will rarely receive more than a few moments' attention from the judge. Training can be initiated by attaching a training cage, of similar dimensions to a show cage, to the front of stock cages, so that the birds are allowed to enter the training cage if they wish – a small titbit should soon tempt their curiosity. Zebra Finches will also need some time in a separate show cage, being put up in pairs just as though they were being exhibited. However, in Britain it is only permissible by law to keep birds in a show cage for up to one hour in any given twenty-four hour period, unless they are actually in the process of being staged at a competitive exhibition. Therefore, it is necessary to train birds by means of frequent short periods, rather than allowing them to sample show cages for longer periods. While in the show cages, birds should also be placed in a carrying case, moved to another location, removed, and given time to settle. This will give them the opportunity to experience some of the conditions they are bound to meet when being exhibited.

When training birds, it is advisable not actually to train them in show pairs, that is to say, specific cocks and hens which are intended to be exhibited as a pair on the show bench. In order to be successful at the highest level, it is usually necessary to bench birds which display while being judged. Displaying enhances their apparent type and size, making them much more likely to be highly placed in their class. Birds which are used to one another's company will not display as much as birds that are total strangers. It is often necessary to change partners during the show season so that the birds do not become too complacent towards each other as the season progresses.

Matching Birds

An important aspect of exhibiting when showing pairs, rather than single birds, is the matching of the birds which go to make up an exhibit. In order to stage a good pair, the two birds selected must match for shape, shade of colour and size. When these features are matched, the pair is presented as a balanced unit and the birds complement each other rather than highlighting any faults which may be displayed by their partners. For example, if a bird is of good general shape, but tends to carry its tail at not quite a high enough angle, this fault will be made less obvious when it is partnered by a bird with the same imperfect tail carriage, whereas a better bird, with the correct tail carriage, will emphasise the fault. Similarly, with colour, a

Young C.F.W. Zebra Finches receiving initial show training by being allowed free access to an old show cage positioned over the door of their stock cage

bird which is a little too pale will look worse if partnered by a bird of excellent colour on the show bench. Quite often the best matched pairs consist of nest mates. While they should not be used as a breeding pair, there is nothing to prevent very closely related birds being exhibition partners.

For the beginner, when birds are successful on the show bench, there is a temptation to exhibit them at every possible opportunity. Birds should never be overshown, otherwise they become tired, fail to display their true potential on the show bench and often disappoint during the breeding season. It is unwise to exhibit specific birds at more than five one-day shows, or three two-day shows, during the course of one show season.

One must always bear in mind that the cage in which birds are exhibited is part of the exhibit. Dirty or badly maintained cages will often be penalised. Show cages usually require repainting annually, and should be cleaned out each time they have been used. When cleaning cages, remember to inspect the cavity between the false roof and the top, as this is often a favourite haunt of spiders, and few judges will be impressed by being covered in cobwebs. A well-prepared cage can enhance the appearance of any birds, but a dirty or badly painted cage will only reflect badly on the birds within the cage and on the person who benched the exhibit in such a poor state.

Good exhibition preparation is the secret of success on the show bench. Fanciers who consistently bench pairs of well-trained birds, in good condition and in well-maintained cages, will have their share of success. Those who pay little attention to the preparation and presentation of their birds rarely manage to win the top awards.

A pair of C.F.W.s in a standard Z.F.S. show cage. They only require the addition of their cage label before being ready for exhibition

10 Records

Anyone who breeds livestock should always keep accurate written records of all the youngsters he or she produces. No matter for what purpose birds are being bred, it is extremely difficult to formulate a good breeding programme without such a source of information. It may seem quite easy to remember which young were bred from which birds when first starting, but with the passage of time and increases in stock, parentage can be more difficult to recall. Sooner or later, inappropriate individuals are inadvertently mated together, resulting in undesirable colour combinations, poor quality young, or birds which have congenital physical disorders.

Exactly what sort of records are to be kept depends on the personal needs of each birdkeeper. Those who simply wish to keep a mixed collection in a garden aviary will usually only require details of the birds mated together, the young produced and the means of identifying these youngsters. This is the most important type of record to keep and all breeders should have a permanent record of every pairing made. This should specify the pairing used, the young they produced and any other relevent information, such as poor fertility, poor hatchibility, etc. Detailed below is an example of the breeding record sheets I use. While other breeders will use different layouts, their record sheets should contain very similar information. (See Table 1.)

It will be noted that, in addition to using numbered close rings, birds are also fitted with coloured split rings. This provides for easy identification of parentage, eliminating the need to catch up youngsters in order to read ring numbers.

It will be necessary, when looking further back into the parentage of birds, to examine breeding sheets for different years. To overcome this, breeders may like to keep separate record sheets for each individual bird retained. All, or part, of such a record may be shown as in Table 2.

Table 1

CAGE NO: *8*   DATE PAIRED TOGETHER: *12–3–86*

COCK: *Normal/Fawn*	HEN: *Fawn*
YEAR RING: *1985 B201–17*	YEAR RING: *1985 B201–20*
SPLIT RING: *Orange*	SPLIT RING: *Dark Blue*
FIRST ROUND	*SECOND ROUND*
First Egg Laid: *22–3–86*	First Egg Laid: *7–5–86*
Started Sitting: *24–3–86*	Started Sitting: *9–5–86*
First Egg Hatched: *6–4–86*	First Egg Hatched: *24–5–86*
Year Ring Numbers: *22,23,24,38, 49 & 50*	Year Ring Numbers: *82,83,84,85, 96 & 98*

NOTES: *Two fertile eggs from first round transferred to Cage 16.*
Two fertile eggs from second round transferred to Cage 3.
Insufficient Orange & White rings, two young rung with Red & Yellow split rings

DETAILS OF YOUNG

YEAR RING	COLOUR	SEX	SPLIT RING	NOTES
B201–22	FAWN	HEN	Orange & White	Sold
B201–23	NORMAL	HEN	Orange & White	Sold – Claw missing
B201–24	FAWN	HEN	Orange & White	Sold
B201–38	NORMAL	HEN	Orange & White	Sold
B201–49	NORMAL	HEN	Orange & White	Fostered – Sold
B201–50	NORMAL	HEN	Orange & White	Fostered – Sold
B201–82	FAWN	COCK	Orange & White	Sold
B201–83	FAWN	HEN	Orange & White	Sold
B201–84	FAWN	HEN	Orange & White	Retained
B201–85	NORMAL	HEN	Red & Yellow	Retained
B201–96	NORMAL/ FAWN	COCK	Orange & White	Fostered – Sold
B201–98	NORMAL	HEN	Red & Yellow	Fostered – Retained

Table 2

INDIVIDUAL ZEBRA FINCH RECORD CARDS				
YR BRED	COLOUR FORM	SEX	YEAR RING	SPLIT RING

TYPE	COLOUR QUALITY	MARKINGS	FEATHER QUALITY

FATHER		MOTHER	
COLOUR FRM: YEAR BRED: YEAR RING: SPLIT RING:	TYPE: COLOUR: MRKINGS: FEATHER:	COLOUR FRM: YEAR BRED: YEAR RING: SPLIT RING:	TYPE COLOUR: MRKINGS: FEATHER:
PAT. G'FATHER	PAT. G'MOTHER	MAT. G'FATHER	MAT. G'MOTHER
COLOUR: YEAR BRED: YEAR RING: SP. RING:	COLOUR: YEAR BRED: YEAR RING: SP. RING:	COLOUR: YEAR BRED: YEAR RING: SP. RING:	COLOUR: YEAR BRED: YEAR RING: SP. RING:

BRIEF BREEDING RECORDS

YEAR	MATE	YOUNG PRODUCED

BREEDING
  NOTES

BRIEF EXHIBITION RECORDS

1st	2nd	3rd	BEST OF COL.	ADULT ROS.	B'DER ROS.	BEST IN SECT.	BEST ZEBRAS

SONS					DAUGHTERS				
1st	2nd	3rd	AD.ROS.	BR.ROS.	1st	2nd	3rd	AD.ROS.	BR.ROS.

FATHER			BROTHERS & SISTERS			MOTHER		
1st	AD.ROS.	BR.ROS.	1st	AD.ROS.	BR.ROS.	1st	AD.ROS.	BR.ROS.

It would be very time consuming to keep records of this type by conventional methods. However, with the increase in home computers, it is now possible to maintain very detailed records and up-date them easily, as and when required.

Other records one might like to keep could be of specific exhibition results. A suitable layout for this type of record would be Table 3.

Table 3

SHOW: TOTAL ZEBRA FINCH ENTRY:

CLASS	ENTRY	POSN	COCK	HEN	SPECIALS

Or one could perhaps keep a record of the points gained during any particular show season as in Table 4.

Table 4

SHOW	NORMALS	PIEDS	WHTES	ADULTS	B'DERS	TOTAL
TOTAL POINTS						

Obviously, records in themselves do not produce good quality birds. However, when they are used in conjunction with sound practical management and an 'eye' for a good bird, they can greatly assist fanciers in making the right decisions with regard to selecting the best birds to mate to each other.

11 Type

Over the past twenty years, type has become increasingly important and, apart from condition, it is undoubtedly the single most important factor in virtually all varieties of type standard exhibition birds.

Type is the term used to describe the shape of birds, and for anyone who hopes to establish an exhibition quality stud of birds, it is essential that they can differentiate between good and bad type. When a reasonably large number of the same birds are being shown in competitive exhibition, it is usually necessary to decide which shape of bird is to be preferred and therefore a type standard will be introduced.

Having decided that it is necessary to adopt a type standard for any particular species or fancy, the next question is what sort of type standard should be introduced. Many fancies use a written standard, in conjunction with an artist's impression of the 'ideal bird'. This may seem quite logical, but, unfortunately, pictorial models will, in the fullness of time, become out-dated. The artist usually depicts a bird of the best possible type, based on the birds currently being bred. However, within a few years specialist breeders will have produced birds which display more desirable type qualities than the pictorial ideal. This inevitably means that a new pictorial ideal must be produced, then further 'improvements' are made, and so it goes on, with every new model being surpassed.

Wisely, the Zebra Finch Society adopts only a written type standard, from which breeders and exhibitors can formulate in their own minds the shape of bird which is desired. Had a pictorial ideal been adopted back in 1952, when the Z.F.S. was founded, this would have needed to be redrawn many times, s the type quality of Zebra Finches has improved over the years. The written standard has, however, remained

The profile outline of what would generally be regarded as good 'cobby' type in finch-like birds. Ideally a Zebra Finch which is not displaying and adopting a natural relaxed stance, should have a similar profile outline to this shape or type

The profile outline one would expect a Zebra Finch, of the type described on the left, to adopt when displaying. At the highest level of competition, unless birds display while being judged, they are unlikely to gain any major awards

The profile outline of a bird which has many attributes associated with good type, but is spoilt by the head being too small. This accentuates the size of the beak, making it appear too large and gives the bird a rather pinched neck. When displaying the bird will tend to mask these faults to some degree

The profile outline of a bird which again has many attributes of good type, but is spoilt by having an excessively flat head. This fault also accentuates the apparent size of the beak and therefore destroys the balance of the bird

The profile outline of a bird with reasonably good type character-istics, spoilt by being 'hollow backed', a fault often associated with birds which have 'crossed wings'. Being hollow backed can sometimes emphasise the head qual-ities, making them appear better than they really are

The profile outline of a bird with good head and neck characteristics which lacks sufficient depth of body, being too slim. Birds of this type often appear greatly improved when displaying and fit birds, in good feather condition, can some-times be more highly placed on the show bench than expected

The profile outline of a bird with good head and body characteristics, totally spoilt by very poor tail car-riage. This is a common feature of birds which have been overshown and in hens, it can be caused by them being about to lay. Any birds showing such poor tail carriage under normal circumstances should not be used to breed exhibition stock, no matter what other virtues they may possess

The outline of a very poor specimen with regard to type. There is no merit whatsoever in any feature of this shape and it would be extrem-ely difficult to build stock of this type up to exhibition standard unchanged since its introduction and still portrays an ideal which is relevant today. The type standard is as follows:

TYPE   Bold throughout and of 'Cobby' type, giving the birds a look of substance; wings evenly carried to root of tail.

Cobby

The only word perhaps requiring further explanation in this standard is 'Cobby'. By using the term cobby, it is hoped to give the impression of a well-rounded bird whose general outline and shape does not display any angularity. This roundness applies to both the head and body, and any features which spoil the outline, such as flat heads, sharpness under the beak, pinched necks, square chests, drooping tails, or a general lack of substance, are to be regarded as type faults. Additionally, features such as crossed wings, dropped wings, hollow backs and poor stance also constitute serious faults. Although the profile of a bird is the most important outline, one should never overlook the width of a bird when viewed face on. A good exhibition Zebra Finch must have plenty of width between the eyes, be full chested and appear solid and compact. Any narrowness between the eyes will give the birds a mean expression.

So how do we start to assess type? It is human nature, when looking at any form of living creature to try to establish eye contact. Most people prefer to see large round bright eyes which tend to be associated with friendliness and honesty. Should the eyes appear disproportionately small, or misshapen, then the over-all impression will be less pleasing visually. After making eye contact, we move on to look at the head. Usually we tend to look for birds with large heads which also display roundness and symmetry, both from front to back and from side to side. It is no coincidence that human babies and children have large heads compared to the size of their bodies, and it is essential for their well being and care that this feature is generally found to be pleasing to adults. The beak of the Zebra Finch is the last feature of the head to be considered. Should this be too large, it will reduce the apparent size of the head and detract from the over-all appearance. A short conical beak which complements the head and does not show any excessive curvature, is usually preferred.

Moving from the head, we then examine the neck. In Zebra Finches this should be solid, but just discernible, between the back of the head and the body in a relaxed bird. When the bird displays, the neck will become 'filled in', so that the head and body blend together with no obvious join between the two. Birds which display continually usually give an enhanced impression of their type and in order to assess the type of any bird accurately, it must be viewed when adopting its normal posture.

The body is the next feature to consider and this will be affected by the stance of the bird. Ideally Zebra Finches should stand so that the back is at an angle of about 45° to the vertical. Birds that crouch will seldom appear to be of good type, while those which stand slightly more erect than normal can enhance their apparent type. The body of a good exhibition Zebra Finch must be well rounded, to present nice clean lines from the base of the beak through to the vent. The back should not be hollow and ideally will have a slightly convex outline as it rises from the neck over the shoulders. In order to 'finish' the body, the wings must be carried evenly and neatly to the base of the tail.

Many potentially good birds have been spoilt by their tail carriage. A drooping tail will destroy the balanced appearance of any Zebra Finch. Ideally the tail should be at a slightly more horizontal angle than the back, but may be carried at the same angle as the back, so that the back and tail form a straight line, without being too detrimental. The tail itself must be neat and tight, and not too long, if it is going to accentuate the desired 'cobby' type.

The final feature to consider are the feet and legs. Although these, in themselves, cannot affect the over-all shape, they can help to emphasise good type. A bird which seems to grip the perch tightly, and has plenty of 'bounce', will appear bolder than those that simply seem to be resting on the perch. If birds lack body, they will often be described as 'leggy'. When a Zebra Finch of good type adopts its normal stance, usually little more than the feet and the bottom part of the legs will be visible. Drawings of Zebra Finches often depict the angle of the leg, between the foot and knee, as being about 45° to the vertical. In point of fact, when sitting on a level perch, the angle of the leg between the foot and knee, in the majority of

Zebra Finches, is very close to being horizontal. The lift, which raises the bird clear of the perch, comes from the angle between the knee and the hip, a part of the leg which should not be visible.

When starting a stud of exhibition birds, it is essential to establish the right type in your stock. Poor shape is one of the most difficult features to correct in livestock. It is much better to get the shape right first and then try to improve the other features later. As yet I have not mentioned size and this is because size does not necessarily have any bearing on shape. Given two pairs of Zebra Finches which are identical in every respect, except for size, it is accepted that the bigger birds are the best. But size should only enter into the judgement when all other features are equal. Nowhere in the standard does it state birds must be big in order to win awards, and size, without good type, colour and markings, should in no way be rewarded on the show bench.

Size

Having said size is not an essential requirement, in order to be successful in the highest levels of competition, it is usually necessary to produce reasonably big birds of good type. This is simply because other exhibitors have already achieved this goal, and it is against these birds that you must eventually compete. In my experience, when trying to increase size without losing type, the best results have been obtained by pairing big hens to cocks of good shape. Youngsters often seem to display the type of their father and the size of their mother. Naturally, when breeding from birds which were produced from stock with some type faults, care must be taken to ensure they are not mated to birds with the same faults as their parents, otherwise these undesirable features will become established in the stud. I would advise that the use of birds with small, flat, or narrow heads, large beaks, a crouching stance, dropped wings or drooping tails, as breeding stock, should be avoided at all times. Occasionally, square-chested hens, which have no other serious type faults, will prove to be useful stock birds, producing young with excellent head qualities.

Until a fancier is able to visualise good type in his or her own mind, there is little chance of being able to establish a top line stud. One of the greatest assets to the breeder of exhibition birds is the mental picture of the 'ideal bird' which can be brought to mind at any time and in any place. This enables the fancier accurately to assess the type qualities of any individual bird, whether he or she is at home, or in the birdroom of another breeder.

Although the physical structure of the skeleton and body is largely responsible for the shape of a bird, it should not be forgotten that feather quality also plays a part in determining the visual type of all birds. Assessing birds by visual type alone is not sufficient, attention must also be paid to feather quality.

12 Feather Quality

It is soon apparent, once birds have been selectively bred for a few generations, that there are two distinct styles of feather. The plumage of some birds is finely structured and displays quite intense colour, while others have broader feathers which show less colour pigmentation. These two styles are generally referred to as 'yellow' and 'buff', with fine-feathered birds being yellows and coarser-feathered birds being buffs. In the wild, the majority of birds are usually yellows, with only a small percentage having buff feathering. The yellow type of feather is genetically dominant, but because many yellows carry the gene for buff feathers hidden in their make-up, a pair consisting of two yellows can produce some buff youngsters. Pairings between a yellow and buff will, on average, produce 50 per cent yellows and 50 per cent buffs, while two buffs can only produce buff-feathered youngsters.

The two styles of feather not only affect visual intensity and evenness of colour in birds, they also play a large part in the type or shape of birds. Yellow-feathered birds, although quite brightly coloured, will usually lack the bold type required in exhibition Zebra Finches, whereas buff-feathered birds which do not display quite such deepness and evenness of colour, tend to be of a bolder and cobbier type. Because buffs often appear to be physically superior to yellows, many of the buffs that are bred tend to be retained. This means that within captive stocks of birds, which are prolific breeders, buffs are just as common as yellows. Where an exhibition type standard exists, and buffs and yellows are exhibited in the same classes, it should come as no surprise to find that most of the successful show birds are buff-feathered.

One might well be excused for thinking that in order to breed exhibition quality birds, the first step is to acquire a stud comprised totally of buff-feathered birds. This is in fact not

A pair of exhibition Fawn Zebra Finches. These birds are examples of buff-feathered birds

the case, as when buffs are mated to buffs for several consecutive generations, the apparent size of the birds bred decreases, shape tends to be lost and the plumage often loses its neatness. The answer is to find a balance between the number of buff-feathered and yellow-feathered birds maintained within a stud. Buff-feathered birds bred from buff x yellow matings can be just as good, if not better, for both type and size, as birds bred from buff x buff pairings. Ideally, when two buff birds are mated together, usually termed as 'double buffing', it is best to use buffs bred from buff x yellow matings. Any young produced as a result of double buffing should, if at all possible, be mated back to yellow-feathered birds. Yellow x yellow pairings are rarely used, the only possible benefit being to improve colour intensity and evenness.

There is no reason why a top quality stud cannot be established and maintained simply by mating buff-feathered birds to yellow-feathered birds. Many breeders fall down by keeping only the largest, best type birds they produce each season, and these will, in the majority of cases, be buff-feathered birds. All may go well for two or three seasons, then the birds start to deteriorate, losing both type and quality, resulting in any progress made being lost. It can be very hard to persuade oneself to keep visually smaller birds, rather than the biggest birds, in order to maintain the balance between buffs and yellows. It is quite possible for yellow-feathered birds to be of good type, although most will lack size, and a yellow of good type can be every bit as useful as a top quality buff in the breeding room. Once established, a good quality stud of Zebra Finches should contain at least 25 per cent yellow-feathered birds.

Birds which have been well established as exhibition type fancy specimens for many, many years, such as Canaries, will usually show a very marked difference between the two types of feather, and close examination of individual feathers will reveal whether they came from buffs or yellows. Zebra Finches, however, have not been established as avicultural subjects for such a long period of time and therefore examination of individual feathers is less conclusive. Some Zebra Finches will obviously be buffs, and others definite yellows, by their visual type, size and colour, but many are not so easily categorised. In such cases, to determine whether Zebra Finches are buff-feathered or yellow-feathered, it is necessary to compare their visual size to their actual size. This is best done by splitting your birds into families and examining batches of brothers and sisters. Starting with the largest visual specimen, catch up all the birds, one by one, and as they are handled, gauge the actual size of each bird by their bulk in your hand. The largest visual specimen will, in the vast majority of cases, be a buff, as will any that look to be a good size but 'feel' smaller, while any which 'feel' to be about the same size, but look smaller, are generally yellows. Birds which look small, feel small and lack good type, will be of little interest to the specialist breeder of exhibition stock.

When first starting to keep Zebra Finches, it may well be that all the birds will look very similar with regard to type and size. As one becomes more familiar with the stock, and accustomed to looking for specific good and bad points, the birds become recognisable as individuals. In the fullness of time it should be possible to identify birds purely by their

This C.F.W. cock was a member of the pair which won the Best Champion Breeder award at the 1976 S.Z.F.S. Club Show. It is an example of a yellow-feathered bird which was good enough to win major honours on the show bench

visual appearance alone, without reference to breeding records and ring numbers. Experience is the best teacher and it is wrong to think anyone can become an expert simply on theoretical knowledge alone. Indeed it is a brave person who would call himself or herself an expert in the field of bird-keeping, as we are all continually seeking new knowledge and learning new lessons. Given time and enthusiasm, it will soon become second nature to categorise stock as either yellow or buff, and once this has been achieved, the planning of breeding programmes can be so much more effective.

13 Inheritance

When breeding any form of livestock, it is an advantage to have at least a rudimentary knowledge of the methods by which different features are inherited. With this knowledge it is possible to calculate which pairings are most likely to produce youngsters of a specific colour, or determine the best methods of trying to establish desirable characteristics in a stud of exhibition birds. In order to predict the inheritance of colour mutations and other features, a little understanding of basic genetics is required. The term genetics covers a very wide and complex field, but we need only uncover the tip of this subject. Unfortunately, many people switch off as soon as the word genetics is mentioned, assuming they will never understand what is to follow. The subject, as far as we are concerned, is much less complicated than generally imagined.

The first reason for being confused by genetics is that two additional terms, chromosomes and genes, are mentioned as soon as any explanation is attempted. These words do represent very complex systems, but, for our basic understanding, it is only necessary to interpret them in very simple terms. Every living creature contains a number of different chromosomes which are arranged in matched pairs. These chromosomes can be regarded simply as a set of instructions, telling the organism how to grow and therefore, among other things, determining its final appearance. The presence of chromosomes is the reason why two very similar eggs, say a Bengalese egg and a Zebra Finch egg, will, on hatching, grow into different birds. The difference between the two eggs is the chromosomes, or instructions within them.

Chromosomes
The chromosomes come from the parents of the embryo: the sperm cells from the father and the unfertilised eggs of the

A nest of young Normals, but one chick is showing some white feathering on the head and is therefore a Normal Pied. There is also a likelihood that its brothers and sisters, although not visually Pieds, will be carrying the mutant gene for Pied hidden in their genetic make-up

mother both contain half a complete set of chromosomes. When the two sets of chromosomes meet, apart from one pair, all form exactly matched physical pairs. The pair which do not match physically are those that determine the sex of the embryo produced, often referred to as the X and Y chromosomes, and these will be dealt with a little more fully later. Until the two sets of chromosomes meet and match up into pairs, no development can take place. Once an embryo is formed, all the information it requires to develop to maturity is contained within its chromosomes. Although the exact number of chromosomes in Zebra Finches has not been determined, there are probably about twenty pairs, contained within each individual body cell.

167

Each separate piece of information contained within a chromosome is referred to as a gene. If we represent a chromosome as being a string of random letters, e.g.

S O L G T P F I N B M R D E W Q A X

and each one of these letters is a separate piece of information, each single letter would be one gene. Now, if we imagine the vast quantity of information needed to be stored within each complete set of chromosomes, and consider they are so small as to be invisible to the naked eye, it is no surprise that genes occasionally contain the wrong information. A gene which varies from the 'normal' gene is known as a mutant gene, and these are responsible for the production of mutations. There are many mutations which we do not want to breed, those, for example, which result in birds having congenital defects. Unless, by means of selective breeding, we attempt to isolate a mutation, it will only occur very rarely. This is because embryos are the product of two sets of chromosomes, one from the father and one from the mother. Where selection is completely random, it is unlikely that the two sets of chromosomes, although they both contain mutant genes, will contain the same mutant genes. In many cases, unless both chromosomes of one pair within an embryo contain the same mutant gene, the 'normal' state will prevail. Let us represent a perfectly formed chromosome which contains no mutant genes, by the following string of letters:

A S B G R T Y H U J I O L M N R D W P

and suppose it is to be partnered by the following chromosome:

A S B K R T Y H U J I O L M N R D W P

These are identical except for the fourth letter which in the normal state is G and in the abnormal state is K. If the letter G tells the developing embryo that each foot has four claws, and K tells it that each foot has five claws, because G is the 'normal' state, it will usually prevail and the embryo will have four claws on each foot. These two chromosomes will then combine to form the following single pair:

A S B G R T Y H U J I O L M N R D W P
A S B K R T Y H U J I O L M N R D W P

When this embryo develops and passes on its own set of chromosomes, either in sperm cells or in eggs, half will contain the normal information and half will contain the 'errant' K factor for deformed feet. Unless this errant gene matches up to another identical gene, in exactly the same position, within one pair of chromosomes, birds with five claws will never be produced. When two identical mutant genes have coincided and a mutation is produced, if it is an undesirable feature, the birds are culled and we selectively breed to prevent these mutant genes meeting in future. Should the mutation be desirable, say a new colour or good exhibition feature, then we retain the birds produced and try to establish the mutation.

If a bird of a new mutation is mated to unrelated birds, it is unlikely that these birds will carry the same mutant gene and it appears that our 'new find' has been lost. But because every embyro contains chromosomes from both the father and mother, we know that these birds will be 'carrying' the mutation. If we mate together two birds that 'carry' the new mutation, there is a chance some embryos will be produced which contain the same mutant gene within both members of one pair of chromosomes. When this occurs, our new mutation will reappear. In fact, in matings of this type, there is a 25 per cent chance of mutants being produced, while a further 50 per cent of the young should carry the mutation but appear as normal, and the remaining 25 per cent should be 'pure bred' and not carry the mutation at all. Now we have a problem: which of the visually normal birds are carrying the mutation and which are not? There is no way to be sure of this by visual inspection; the only possible method is to test mate the birds and see what sort of young are produced. This type of inheritance is known as **recessive** and it is the most usual form. Visual examples of a recessive mutation cannot carry, hidden in their genetic make-up, genes which are dominant to that mutation.

Occasionally a mutant gene arises which is **dominant** to the normal gene present within a chromosome. In such cases, once the mutant gene is present in an embryo, it will be shown visually by the embryo when it develops. Let us represent a 'normal' chromosome by the following string of letters:

W P O V Q J Z

and the same chromosome, containing a dominant mutant gene, by the following string of letters:

W C O V Q J Z

with the mutation occurring on the second letter, and P being replaced by C. Because C takes precedence over P when they meet in an embryo, any embryo with this combination of chromosomes will develop in accordance with the information contained in C. Although the embryo will visually display the characteristics of C, it also contains a chromosome which carries the 'normal' gene P, and would be described as a single factor or (s.f.) example of the mutation. Such birds can pass on to their offspring both 'normal' chromosomes, i.e.

W P O V Q J Z

or chromosomes containing the mutant gene, i.e.

W C O V Q J Z

Whenever this mutant gene occurs within an embryo, it will be manifested in the individual formed. Should two individuals be mated together which both carry the mutant gene C, the following pair of chromosomes would, theoretically, be present in 25 per cent of the embryos produced:

W C O V Q J Z

W C O V Q J Z

Every set of chromosomes produced by a bird developed from such an embryo will contain C, and individuals of this type would be described as double factor or (d.f.) examples of the mutation. All the young produced from such a bird would visually display the characteristics of C. Birds with a 'double dose' of C will not differ visually from single factor examples of the mutation, the only difference is in the chromosomes they produce. This is the dominant method of inheritance and it is impossible for a dominant mutation to be carried in hidden form. Dominant mutations sometimes carry a lethal factor which means that the double factor embryos become unviable and will die during some stage in their development.

X and Y Chromosomes

The previous situations will, however, differ when mutant

genes are contained within the sex chromosomes. In birds, males contain two X chromosomes and females contain one X and one Y chromosome, and this factor determines the sex of each individual bird. Interestingly, in humans it is males which contain an X and Y chromosome and females which have two X chromosomes, exactly opposite to the situation in birds. When an X chromosome from a cock bird and an X chromosome from a hen meet in an embryo, that embryo will be a cock. If an X chromosome from the cock meets with a Y chromosome from the hen, the embryo produced will be a female. In theory there is exactly a 50/50 chance of cocks or hens being produced. Here X and Y are used to represent whole chromosomes:

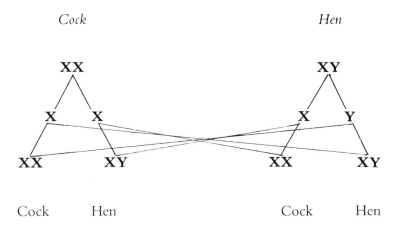

Cock　　　　　　　　　　　　　　　　*Hen*

XX　　　　　　　　　　　　　　　　**XY**

X　　**X**　　　　　　　　　　**X**　　**Y**

XX　　**XY**　　　　　　**XX**　　**XY**

Cock　　Hen　　　　　　Cock　　Hen

The Y chromosome, however, can be regarded as carrying no other information apart from determining the sex of the embryo formed. Therefore, when a mutant gene occurs on the X chromosome, and that chromosome pairs with a Y chromosome, there is no 'normal' gene available to 'correct' the mutant. This means that the female embryos which contain mutant genes on their X chromosome will develop in accordance with the information given by the mutant gene. Where two X chromosomes form a pair and one contains a mutant gene, their interaction usually follows either the recessive or dominant pattern of inheritance. In the majority of cases the mutant genes will be recessive, and mutations of this type are referred to as being recessive sex-linked or simply,

sex-linked. When a recessive sex-linked cock is mated to a 'normal' hen, all the hens produced will be of the sex-linked mutation and all the cock birds will be visually 'normal', but will carry the sex-linked mutation in their make-up. If a cock bird, which does not visually show a sex-linked mutation, produces any young hens which are visual examples of a sex-linked mutation, he must be carrying the mutant gene responsible for that mutation 'hidden' in his genetic make-up. This rule applies in all cases, regardless of the genetic make-up of the hen mated to the cock. It will be found that many cock Zebra Finches carry sex-linked mutant colour genes in their make-up.

When a hen of a recessive sex-linked mutation is mated to a pure 'normal' cock, all the hens produced will be pure 'normal' and the cocks will be visually 'normal' but carry the sex-linked factor in their genetical make-up. It is impossible for hens to carry a sex-linked mutation in hidden form; if the mutation is present in their make-up, then they will, in fact, be visual examples of that mutation. In order to produce a cock bird of a recessive sex-linked mutation, it is necessary for its mother to be a visual example of that mutation and also for its father to at least 'carry' the sex-linked mutation in his genetic make-up. If a dominant mutant gene was located on the X chromosome this would give rise to a dominant sex-linked mutation. This is not particularly applicable to Zebra Finches currently, and any reference to sex-linked mutations should be regarded as the recessive form.

Another type of inheritance exists where there is no definite dominance between two different genes that occur on the same position within one pair of chromosomes. In such cases the resulting embryo will develop some features of both genes or appear to be an intermediate state between the two mutants. This type of inheritance is known as **incomplete dominance**.

We have considered what happens when mutations are mated to the 'normal' form, or the same two mutations are mated together. Now we will consider what occurs when two different mutations meet within the same embryo. Because the mutations are produced by different mutant genes which usually occur on totally different chromosomes, the result is to produce offspring which visually revert back to being of 'normal' appearance. Let us assume that we have two recessive mutations which occur due to the presence of mutant genes on two different pairs of chromosomes. We will represent the 'normal' appearance of the two particular pairs in which we are interested by the following two strings of letters:

```
S G F K T X H        M J Z L R Y N
S G F K T X H        M J Z L R Y N
```

We will call the two recessive mutations A and B, A occurring in the first pair of chromosomes, replacing the 'normal' gene F with the mutant gene A, and B occurring in the second pair of chromosomes, replacing the 'normal' gene R with the mutant gene B. Therefore, in a pure bred specimen which displays the characteristics of mutation A, the two pairs of chromosomes would appear as follows:

```
S G A K T X H        M J Z L R Y N
S G A K T X H        M J Z L R Y N
```

In the case of mutation B the two pairs of chromosomes will appear as:

```
S G F K T X H        M J Z L B Y N
S G F K T X H        M J Z L B Y N
```

When the two mutations are mated together, the result will be to form the following two pairs of chromosomes:

```
S G A K T X H        M J Z L R Y N
S G F K T X H        M J Z L B Y N
```

As the mutant gene A has aligned itself to the 'normal' gene F, and A is a recessive mutation, the embryo formed will adopt the instructions given by gene F. Similarly, because the mutant gene B is aligned to the 'normal' gene R, and B is also a recessive mutation, then the embryo will obey the instructions contained in gene R. The result is that a visually 'normal' youngster is produced, although the embryo contains both mutant gene A and B in its make-up. While mutations A and B are not evident visually, they can be passed on to future generations. Should they coincide with similar recessive mutant genes within chromosomes produced by another bird, they will be displayed visually. Results of this type are the

usual condition when two different pure bred recessive mutations are mated together.

The next situation to consider is the combination of recessive and dominant mutations within the same bird. Again the
mutant genes responsible for these mutations usually occur on
different chromosomes, or on different genes within the same
chromosome. Let us take, for example, the mating of a
recessive mutation A to a dominant mutation C, where the
bird of the dominant mutation is a single factor. Mutation A
will occur on the same chromosome as it did in the previous
example and mutation C will be the same as in the example
originally chosen to illustrate the dominant mutation (see p
169–70). Therefore, in the case of mutation C, the two pairs of
chromosomes in which we are interested, appear as follows.

$$S\ G\ F\ K\ T\ X\ H \qquad W\ C\ O\ V\ Q\ J\ Z$$
$$S\ G\ F\ K\ T\ X\ H \qquad W\ P\ O\ V\ Q\ J\ Z$$

In mutation A the two pairs will appear as:

$$S\ G\ A\ K\ T\ X\ H \qquad W\ P\ O\ V\ Q\ J\ Z$$
$$S\ G\ A\ K\ T\ X\ H \qquad W\ P\ O\ V\ Q\ J\ Z$$

When the two mutations are mated together, the following
two combinations can occur:

$$S\ G\ F\ K\ T\ X\ H \qquad W\ C\ O\ V\ Q\ J\ Z$$
$$S\ G\ A\ K\ T\ X\ H \qquad W\ P\ O\ V\ Q\ J\ Z$$

or

$$S\ G\ F\ K\ T\ X\ H \qquad W\ P\ O\ V\ Q\ J\ Z$$
$$S\ G\ A\ K\ T\ X\ H \qquad W\ P\ O\ V\ Q\ J\ Z$$

In the case of the first group, the embryo produced has A
aligned to F and as A is recessive, F is adopted by the embryo.
The mutant gene C is aligned to 'normal' gene P, but because
C is dominant the embryo will display the visual characteristics of mutation C. In the second group of chromosomes, the
first pair are identical to the first pair in the first group, but the
second pair do not contain the mutant gene C anywhere in
their make-up. Birds carrying the first group of chromosomes
will be visual single factor examples of mutation C and will be
carrying mutant gene A hidden in their genetic make-up.
Birds with the second group of chromosomes also carry the
mutant gene A hidden in their genetic make-up, but do not

carry the mutant gene C at all and must therefore be of 'normal' appearance.

When a pure bred sex-linked mutation and a pure bred recessive non-sex-linked mutation are combined, the results depend upon the sex of the mutations involved. As usual, if a cock of a sex-linked mutation is involved in pairings, all the young hens produced will be visual examples of the sex-linked mutation. When a hen of a sex-linked mutation is mated to a cock which is a visual example of a recessive mutation, then all the hens will be visually 'normal', but will carry the mutant gene for the recessive mutation hidden in their genetic make-up. Hens cannot carry any sex-linked mutation in hidden form. The young cocks produced, when genetically pure birds of both sexes are used, will be of 'normal' appearance but will carry both the sex-linked and recessive mutations hidden in their make-up. Should impure birds be used, i.e. visual examples of sex-linked mutations which carry the recessive mutation in hidden form, or a visual cock of the recessive mutation which is carrying the sex-linked mutation hidden in its genetic make-up, then birds which show the visual characteristics of both mutations may be produced.

If a sex-linked cock and a hen of a non-sex-linked dominant mutation are intermated, and pure bred birds are used, the young hens produced will often be visual examples of both the mutations involved. When the dominant hen is a single factor bird, half the young hens should show this combination, and when the dominant hen is a double factor bird, all the young hens will be combinations of the two mutations. The young cocks produced, whatever their visual characteristics, will be carrying the sex-linked mutation within their genetic make-up. When the sexes in this type of mating are reversed, all the hens produced will be visually either 'normal' or the dominant mutation used and, once again, will not 'carry' the sex-linked mutation. The cocks produced will also be visually 'normal' or visual examples of the dominant mutation, but all will be 'carrying' the mutant gene for the sex-linked mutation hidden in their genetic make-up. When a cock bird of a dominant mutation, which also carries a sex-linked mutation in hidden form, is mated to a hen which is a visual example of the same sex-linked mutation, it is possible to produce some cocks and hens which are visual combinations of the two mutations.

Should two different sex-linked mutations be involved in pairings, a process known as 'crossing over' can lead to unexpected results being obtained. Crossing over is a term applied to the breaking up and recombining of a pair of X chromosomes. If this occurs in a pair of X chromosomes, where each member of the pair contains a mutant gene for a different sex-linked mutation, the result can be to form a pair of X chromosomes consisting of one totally 'normal' chromosome and one chromosome which carries both mutant genes for the two sex-linked mutations involved. Once an X chromosome containing both mutant genes for two different sex-linked mutations has been produced, it is possible to breed birds which will be visual combinations of the two different mutations. In the majority of cases, the first examples of these combined mutations to be produced will be hens, as they only have one X chromosome and this determines their visual appearance with regard to sex-linked mutations. Until a cock is produced which has in its genetic make-up a pair of X chromosomes, both of which contain mutant genes, for both sex-linked mutations, it is impossible for a cock bird to show the combination of the two different mutations visually. Where mutant genes for two different sex-linked mutations occur in exactly the same position on the X chromosome, it is not possible to produce visual combinations of the two mutations involved. No matter how the X chromosomes split and recombine, it is impossible to produce an X chromosome which contains both mutant genes.

Finally, we will consider what happens when two different mutations do occur in the same position on the same chromosome, and this applies to all chromosomes, not just the X chromosome. Let us call two mutations which occur in exactly the same position D and E and represent the chromosome which contains the mutant gene D as follows:

G Y P D H W S

and the chromosome when it contains the mutant gene E as follows:

G Y P E H W S

When the chromosome pairs form, as a result of mating between mutations D and E, the specific chromosome pair we wish to consider will appear thus:

G Y P D H W S
G Y P E H W S

As neither D nor E are the normal genes, youngsters of normal appearance cannot be produced. The exact appearance of the young will depend on the interaction between D and E. One may be dominant to the other, in which case the developing embryo will take on the appearance of the dominant mutant gene. If neither is dominant, it will be a case of incomplete dominance and the embryo will develop characteristics of both mutations. Situations of this kind, where two different mutant genes occur in exactly the same position, are called **allelomorphs** or alleles. Birds which include in their genetical make-up a pair of chromosomes which contain two different mutations in exactly the same position, can pass on chromosomes containing one or other of the mutant genes, but not both in the same chromosome.

With regard to the recognised colours of Zebra Finches, their methods of inheritance are all based on results obtained when they are mated to Normal or Grey Zebras. The only dominant mutation recognised by the Z.F.S. is Dominant Dilute. However, the Black Cheeked mutation is said to be dominant and, in other species, Crested forms are usually dominant, and this may well prove to be the case with Crested Zebra Finches. A double factor of the Dominant Dilute mutation has not proved to be a lethal condition, although a double factor for Crests is usually regarded as being lethal with other species which are normally uncrested. The recognised recessive mutations are Pied, White, Penguin, Yellow-Beak and Recessive Dilute. At least three, as yet unrecognised, mutations, Black Breasted, Orange Breasted and Isabel, are also believed to be recessive mutations. The recognised sex-linked mutations are Fawn, Chestnut Flanked White and Light Back, with Light Backs being a form of sex-linked dilute. There does, however, exist a very close relationship between Chestnut Flanked Whites and Light Backs, and matings between these two mutations seem to indicate the state described for allelomorphs. I also believe that mating results point towards a form of incomplete dominance, as Light Back cocks, which carry the mutant Chestnut Flanked White gene, are of a paler colour than pure Light Back cocks. Where hens are concerned, because the two mutations are sex-linked, they cannot carry genes for both mutations, and it is interesting to note that Light Back hens are generally darker than Light Back cocks. This being the case, it would be the only example of incomplete dominance among the colours of Zebra Finch currently recognised by the Zebra Finch Society.

When a bird is carrying mutant genes, the effects of which are not displayed visually, it is usually said to be 'split' for whatever mutations are being hidden in its genetic make-up. The term split is expressed as: / , with the visual state of the bird being written first and any hidden factors being written second. A Normal Grey cock which is carrying Pied and Penguin hidden in its genetical make-up would appear thus: Normal/Pied and Penguin cock.

The basic rules of genetics can help us in deciding whether or not to inbreed, this being the term for mating together two very closely related individuals. We know that mistakes occur in the genetic make-up of all living creatures. Many of these mistakes would result in undesirable freaks being produced if they ever came to light. There is a much greater chance of breeding these freaks when two closely related birds are intermated, and if the process is continued, the chances are increased once again. Should either of the two closely related birds display any undesirable features, then these are very likely to be manifested in the young produced. These undesirable features need not only be visual characteristics, they may relate to poor egg-laying capacity or the inability to fertilise eggs. Inbreeding does have a place in the production of exhibition quality birds, but only when used thoughtfully on a limited scale.

One of the most successful methods of actually producing new mutations is by allowing very closely related birds to intermate indiscriminately for several successive seasons. All sorts of new mutants may arise, and, occasionally, a new colour will be produced. Having produced birds which visually display a desirable mutant gene, it is a fairly simple matter, knowing the basics of genetics, to establish the new colour form. The fact that mutations can be produced by these indiscriminate pairings perhaps explains why so few mutations appear in British birdrooms. The vast majority of birdkeepers in this country only rarely allow matings such as parents to children or brothers to sisters, to take place.

This chapter may seem to be quite distantly removed from the simple pleasure of keeping birds. A basic understanding of genetics will, however, help you to gain much more satisfaction from your birds and create added interest, especially during the breeding season. I have purposely refrained from using many of the technical terms usually associated with genetics in the hope that my explanations are easier to follow, although they may be rather more long-winded than necessary. However, the old adage that 'you only get out what you put in' rings particularly true. If you put faults into your birds they will inevitably reappear at some time in the future and if you persist in breeding good qualities into your birds, then they are bound to improve.

This nest of young Zebras was bred from a Normal/C.F.W. cock mated to a C.F.W. hen. Such a pairing has the possibility of producing Normal/C.F.W. cocks, C.F.W. cocks, Normal hens and C.F.W. hens. In this case it is likely that the C.F.W. youngster will be a cock, as it has a very light head, but the Normal youngsters may be either Normal/C.F.W. cocks or pure Normal hens

14 Matings and Colour Expectations

It is not my intention here to provide a list of all the possible matings which can be made between different colours of Zebra Finches. A limited number of examples have been provided and, by using these, the expectations from many other pairings can be calculated.

The list of matings is laid out in a uniform pattern. The parents appear on the left and the youngsters which can be produced appear on the right, e.g. Normal x Normal → 100%. The percentages given are based on the results which would be obtained when a very large number of young were bred from a specific pairing. In practical terms, these percentages vary from nest to nest and individual pairs will often produce different percentages in any given breeding season. If it was possible to produce very large numbers of young from one pair, say upwards of 100, it would be found that the practical percentages would conform very closely to the theoretical figures given in this list. Mention of sexes used or produced in matings is only made when this is relevant; where sexes are not mentioned, results will be the same no matter which colour is the cock and which the hen.

The different types of colour inheritance are categorised by results obtained when mutations are mated to the 'normal' form. In Zebra Finches the Normal or Grey is classed as being the normal form. This may seem obvious, but in some species the commonest wild type is not always regarded as being the normal. Where a mutation can occur in different colour forms, those written as the mutation, without reference to other colours, appear as the Normal form of that mutation, i.e. Pied = Normal Pied, Penguin = Normal Penguin, etc. In order to represent birds which are split for other colours, the standard / is used. A visual Normal which carries mutant genes for both Pied and Penguin will be written as: Normal/Pied and Penguin. In all cases the visual appearance of the bird appears on the left and any mutations which are being carried in hidden form appear on the right.

The mating list deals mainly with three types of inheritance, namely recessive, dominant and sex-linked. The recognised colours of Zebra Finch fall into the following categories:

NORMAL: Normal or Grey.

RECESSIVE: Pied, White, Penguin, Yellow-Beak and Recessive Dilute.

DOMINANT: Dominant Dilute.

SEX-LINKED: Fawn, Chestnut Flanked White and Light Back.

Of the colours at present not recognised by the Zebra Finch Society, Black Breasted, Orange Breasted and Isabel are thought to be recessive mutations. Black Cheeked Zebras are thought to be dominant, and in most species of birds the Crested form is usually dominant genetically.

When considering Dominant and Recessive Dilute mutations, remember that the Normal forms of these mutations are known as Silver, but when the mutations are combined visually with the Fawn mutation, they are referred to as Creams. Where Dominant Silvers or Creams are mentioned, (s.f.) denotes single factor birds which carry only one dilute factor in their genetic make-up, and (d.f.) denotes double factor birds which carry two dilute factors in their genetic make-up. It may be helpful to consider single factor Silvers being Silver/Normal and single factor Creams being Cream/Fawn. This is not, in fact, strictly accurate, but may be of use if you are unfamiliar with genetics and the workings of colour expectations.

To determine results from pairings not specifically mentioned in the mating lists, find a mating between colours with the same type of inheritance and substitute the colours given as examples with the colours actually required. For example, if you wish to determine the results from matings between Fawns and Recessive Silvers, locate the section headed Recessive x Sex-Linked. This uses Pied x Fawn matings as examples. To find the results from any specific mating, substitute Pied with Recessive Silver throughout the whole mating, bearing in mind that whenever the appearance of a bird is described as being Fawn Recessive Silver, in place of Fawn

Pied, it will be a Recessive Cream. Should matings between Chestnut Flanked Whites and Penguins be of interest, then Fawn will need to be replaced by Chestnut Flanked White and Pied by Penguin, in order to calculate the results obtained. The term Chestnut Flanked White is, as usual, abbreviated to C.F.W. in the mating list.

Mating Lists and Colour Expectations

Normal x Normal

Normal x Normal	→	100% Normal

Normal x Recessive

Normal x Pied	→	100% Normal/Pied
Normal/Pied x Normal/Pied	→	25% Normal, 50% Normal/Pied, 25% Pied
Normal x Normal/Pied	→	50% Normal, 50% Normal/Pied
Normal/Pied x Pied	→	50% Normal/Pied, 50% Pied
Pied x Pied	→	100% Pied

Normal x Dominant

Normal x Silver (s.f.)	→	50% Normal, 50% Silver (s.f.)
Silver (s.f.) x Silver (s.f.)	→	25% Normal, 50% Silver (s.f.), 25% Silver (d.f.)
Normal x Silver (d.f.)	→	100% Silver (s.f.)
Silver (d.f.) x Silver (s.f.)	→	50% Silver (d.f.), 50% Silver (s.f.)
Silver (d.f.) x Silver (d.f.)	→	100% Silver (d.f.)

Normal x Sex-linked

Normal Cock x Fawn Hen	→	50% Normal/Fawn Cocks, 50% Normal Hens
Fawn Cock x Normal Hen	→	50% Normal/Fawn Cocks, 50% Fawn Hens
Normal/Fawn Cock x Normal Hen	→	25% Normal Cocks, 25% Normal/Fawn Cocks, 25% Normal Hens, 25% Fawn Hens
Normal/Fawn Cock x Fawn Hen	→	25% Normal/Fawn Cocks, 25% Fawn Cocks, 25% Normal Hens, 25% Fawn Hens
Fawn Cock x Fawn Hen	→	100% Fawn Cocks and Hens

Recessive x *Recessive*

Pied x Penguin	→	100% Normal/Pied & Penguin
Normal/Pied & Penguin x Normal/Pied & Penguin	→	6¼% Normal, 12½% Normal/Pied, 12½% Normal/Penguin, 25% Normal/Pied & Penguin, 12½% Pied/Penguin, 12½% Penguin/Pied, 6¼% Pied, 6¼% Penguin, 6¼% Penguin Pied
Normal/Pied & Penguin x Penguin	→	25% Normal/Penguin, 25% Normal/Pied & Penguin, 25% Penguin/Pied, 25% Penguin
Normal/Pied & Penguin x Pied	→	25% Normal/Pied, 25% Normal/Pied & Penguin, 25% Pied/Penguin, 25% Pied
Normal/Pied x Pied/Penguin	→	25% Normal/Pied, 25% Normal/Pied & Penguin, 25% Pied/Penguin, 25% Pied
Normal/Pied x Penguin/Pied	→	25% Normal/Penguin, 50% Normal/Pied & Penguin, 25% Pied/Penguin
Pied/Penguin x Penguin/Pied	→	25% Normal/Pied & Penguin, 25% Pied/Penguin, 25% Penguin/Pied, 25% Penguin Pied
Penguin Pied x Pied	→	100% Pied/Penguin
Pied/Penguin x Pied/Penguin	→	25% Pied, 50% Pied/Penguin, 25% Penguin Pied
Penguin Pied x Pied/Penguin	→	50% Pied/Penguin, 50% Penguin Pied
Penguin Pied x Penguin Pied	→	100% Penguin Pied

Recessive x *Dominant*

Pied x Silver (s.f.)	→	50% Normal/Pied, 50% Silver (s.f.)/Pied
Pied x Silver (d.f.)	→	100% Silver (s.f.)/Pied
Silver (s.f.)/Pied x Pied	→	25% Normal/Pied, 25% Pied, 25% Silver (s.f.)/Pied, 25% Silver (s.f.) Pied
Silver (s.f.)/Pied x Silver (s.f.)/Pied	→	6¼% Normal, 12½% Normal/Pied, 6¼% Pied, 25% Silver (s.f.)/Pied, 12½% Silver (d.f.)/Pied, 12½% Silver (s.f.) Pied, 6¼% Silver (d.f.) Pied, 12½% Silver (s.f.), 6¼% Silver (d.f.)

Silver (d.f.)/Pied x Pied	→	50% Silver (s.f.)/Pied, 50% Silver (s.f.) Pied
Silver (s.f.) Pied x Pied	→	50% Pied, 50% Silver (s.f.) Pied
Silver (s.f.) Pied x Silver (s.f.) Pied	→	25% Pied, 50% Silver (s.f.) Pied, 25% Silver (d.f.) Pied
Silver (d.f.) Pied x Pied	→	100% Silver (s.f.) Pied
Silver (d.f.) Pied x Silver (s.f.) Pied	→	50% Silver (s.f.) Pied, 50% Silver (d.f.) Pied
Silver (d.f.) Pied x Silver (d.f.) Pied	→	100% Silver (d.f.) Pied

Recessive x *Sex-linked*

Fawn Cock x Pied Hen	→	50% Normal/Fawn & Pied Cocks, 50% Fawn/Pied Hens
Pied Cock x Fawn Hen	→	50% Normal/Fawn & Pied Cocks, 50% Normal/Pied Hens
Normal/Fawn & Pied Cock x Fawn/Pied Hen	→	6¼% Normal/Fawn Cocks, 12½% Normal/Fawn & Pied Cocks, 6¼% Fawn Cocks, 12½% Fawn/Pied Cocks, 6¼% Pied/Fawn Cocks, 6¼% Fawn Pied Cocks, 6¼% Normal Hens, 12½% Normal/Pied Hens, 6¼% Fawn Hens, 12½% Fawn/Pied Hens, 6¼% Pied Hens, 6¼% Fawn Pied Hens
Pied Cock x Fawn/Pied Hen	→	25% Normal/Fawn & Pied Cocks, 25% Pied/Fawn Cocks, 25% Normal/Pied Hens, 25% Pied Hens
Pied Cock x Fawn Pied Hen	→	50% Pied/Fawn Cocks, 50% Pied Hens
Pied/Fawn Cock x Pied Hen	→	25% Pied Cocks, 25% Pied/Fawn Cocks, 25% Pied Hens, 25% Fawn Pied Hens
Pied/Fawn Cock x Fawn Hen	→	25% Normal/Fawn & Pied Cocks, 25% Fawn/Pied Cocks, 25% Normal/Pied Hens, 25% Fawn/Pied Hens
Pied/Fawn Cock x Fawn/Pied Hen	→	12½% Normal/Fawn & Pied Cocks, 12½% Fawn/Pied Cocks, 12½% Pied/Fawn Cocks, 12½% Fawn Pied Cocks, 12½% Normal/Pied Hens, 12½% Fawn/Pied Hens, ₁12½% Pied Hens, 12½% Fawn Pied Hens

Pied/Fawn Cock x 　Fawn Pied Hen	→	25% Pied/Fawn Cocks, 25% Fawn 　Pied Cocks, 25% Pied Hens, 25% 　Fawn Pied Hens
Fawn Cock x Fawn Pied Hen	→	100% Fawn/Pied Cocks and Hens
Fawn Cock x Fawn/Pied Hen	→	25% Fawn Cocks, 25% Fawn/Pied 　Cocks, 25% Fawn Hens, 25% 　Fawn/Pied Hens
Fawn/Pied Cock x Pied Hen	→	25% Normal/Fawn & Pied Cocks, 　25% Pied/Fawn Cocks, 25% Fawn/ 　Pied Hens, 25% Fawn Pied Hens
Fawn/Pied Cock x Fawn Hen	→	25% Fawn Cocks, 25% Fawn/Pied 　Cocks, 25% Fawn Hens, 25% 　Fawn/Pied Hens
Fawn/Pied Cock x 　Fawn/Pied Hen	→	12½% Fawn Cocks, 25% Fawn/Pied 　Cocks, 12½% Fawn Pied Cocks, 　12½% Fawn Hens, 25% Fawn/Pied 　Hens, 12½% Fawn Pied Hens
Fawn/Pied Cock x 　Fawn Pied Hen	→	25% Fawn/Pied Cocks, 25% Fawn 　Pied Cocks, 25% Fawn/Pied Hens, 　25% Fawn Pied Hens
Fawn Pied Cock x Pied Hen	→	50% Pied/Fawn Cocks, 50% Fawn 　Pied Hens
Fawn Pied Cock x Fawn Hen	→	100% Fawn/Pied Cocks and Hens
Fawn Pied Cock x 　Fawn/Pied Hen	→	25% Fawn/Pied Cocks, 25% Fawn 　Pied Cocks, 25% Fawn/Pied Hens, 　25% Fawn Pied Hens
Fawn Pied Cock x 　Fawn Pied Hen	→	100% Fawn Pied Cocks and Hens

Dominant x *Sex-linked*

Silver (s.f.) Cock x Fawn Hen	→	25% Normal/Fawn Cocks, 25% Silver 　(s.f.)/ Fawn Cocks, 25% Normal 　Hens, 25% Silver (s.f.) Hens
Silver (d.f.) Cock x 　Fawn Hen	→	50% Silver (s.f.)/Fawn Cocks, 　50% Silver (s.f.) Hens
Fawn Cock x Silver (s.f.) Hen	→	25% Normal/Fawn Cocks, 25% Silver 　(s.f.)/Fawn Cocks, 25% Fawn Hens, 　25% Cream (s.f.) Hens
Fawn Cock x Silver (d.f.) Hen	→	50% Silver (s.f.)/Fawn Cocks, 50% 　Cream (s.f.) Hens
Silver (s.f.)/Fawn Cock x 　Fawn Hen	→	12½% Normal/Fawn Cocks, 12½% 　Fawn Cocks, 12½% Silver (s.f.)/ 　Fawn Cocks, 12½% Cream (s.f.) →

		Cocks, 12½% Normal Hens, 12½% Fawn Hens, 12½% Silver (s.f.) Hens, 12½% Cream (s.f.) Hens
Silver (s.f.)/Fawn Cock x Normal Hen	→	12½% Normal Cocks, 12½% Normal/Fawn Cocks, 12½% Silver (s.f.) Cocks, 12½% Silver (s.f.)/Fawn Cocks, 12¹/2% Normal Hens, 12¹/2% Fawn Hens, 12½% Silver (s.f.) Hens, 12½% Cream (s.f.) Hens
Silver (s.f.)/Fawn Cock x Silver (s.f.) Hen	→	6¼% Normal Cocks, 6¼% Normal/Fawn Cocks, 12½% Silver (s.f.) Cocks, 12½% Silver (s.f.)/Fawn Cocks, 6¼% Silver (d.f.) Cocks, 6¼% Silver (d.f.)/Fawn Cocks, 6¼% Normal Hens, 6¼% Fawn Hens, 12½% Silver (s.f.) Hens, 6¼% Silver (d.f.) Hens, 12½% Cream (s.f.) Hens, 6¼% Cream (d.f.) Hens
Silver (s.f.)/Fawn Cock x Cream (s.f.) Hen	→	6¼% Normal/Fawn Cocks, 6¼% Fawn Cocks, 12½% Silver (s.f.)/Fawn Cocks, 6¼% Silver (d.f.)/ Fawn Cocks, 12½% Cream (s.f.) Cocks, 6¼% Cream (d.f.) Cocks, 6¼% Normal Hens, 6¼% Fawn Hens, 12½% Silver (s.f.) Hens, 6¼% Silver (d.f.) Hens, 12½% Cream (s.f.) Hens, 6¼% Cream (d.f.) Hens
Fawn Cock x Cream (s.f.) Hen	→	25% Fawn Cocks, 25% Cream (s.f.) Cocks, 25% Fawn Hens, 25% Cream (s.f.) Hens
Fawn Cock x Cream (d.f.) Hen	→	100% Cream (s.f.) Cocks and Hens
Cream (s.f.) Cock x Fawn Hen	→	25% Fawn Cocks, 25% Cream (s.f.) Cocks, 25% Fawn Hens, 25% Cream (s.f.) Hens
Cream (d.f.) Cock x Fawn Hen	→	100% Cream (s.f.) Cocks and Hens
Cream (s.f.) Cock x Normal Hen	→	25% Normal/Fawn Cocks, 25% Silver (s.f.)/Fawn Cocks, 25% Fawn Hens, 25% Cream (s.f.) Hens
Cream (d.f.) Cock x Normal Hen	→	50% Silver (s.f.)/Fawn Cocks, 50% Cream (s.f.) Hens
Normal Cock x Cream (s.f.) Hen	→	25% Normal/Fawn Cocks, 25% Silver (s.f.)/Fawn Cocks, 25% Normal Hens, 25% Silver (s.f.) Hens

Normal Cock x
  Cream (d.f.) Hen
→ 50% Silver (s.f.)/Fawn Cocks, 50% Silver (s.f.) Hens

Normal/Fawn Cock x
  Cream (s.f.) Hen
→ 12½% Normal/Fawn Cocks, 12½% Fawn Cocks, 12½% Silver (s.f.)/Fawn Cocks, 12½% Cream (s.f.) Cocks, 12½% Normal Hens, 12½% Fawn Hens, 12½% Silver (s.f.) Hens, 12½% Cream (s.f.) Hens

Normal/Fawn Cock x
  Silver (s.f.) Hen
→ 12½% Normal Cocks, 12½% Normal/Fawn Cocks, 12½% Silver (s.f.)/Fawn Cocks, 12½% Silver (s.f.) Cocks, 12½% Normal Hens, 12½% Fawn Hens, 12½% Silver (s.f.) Hens, 12½% Cream (s.f.) Hens

Cream (s.f.) Cock x
  Silver (s.f.) Hen
→ 12½% Normal/Fawn Cocks, 25% Silver (s.f.)/Fawn Cocks, 12½% Silver (d.f.)/Fawn Cocks, 12½% Fawn Hens, 25% Cream (s.f.) Hens, 12½% Cream (d.f.) Hens

Silver (s.f.) Cock x
  Cream (s.f.) Hen
→ 12½% Normal/Fawn Cocks, 25% Silver (s.f.)/Fawn Cocks, 12½% Silver (d.f.)/Fawn Cocks, 12½% Normal Hens, 25% Silver (s.f.) Hens, 12½% Silver (d.f.) Hens

Cream (s.f.) Cock x
  Cream (s.f.) Hen
→ 25% Fawn Cocks and Hens, 50% Cream (s.f.) Cocks and Hens, 25% Cream (d.f.) Cocks and Hens

Cream (d.f.) Cock x
  Cream (s.f.) Hen
→ 50% Cream (s.f.) Cocks and Hens, 50% Cream (d.f.) Cocks and Hens

Cream (d.f.) Cock x
  Cream (d.f.) Hen
→ 100% Cream (d.f.) Cocks and Hens

Sex-linked x Sex-linked

Due to the nature of the effect known as 'crossing over', where X chromosomes split and then recombine, any percentages given for some of the colours produced in these matings would be arbitrary. Percentages are therefore omitted unless they are definitely of known values. Where it is believed that the percentage of a certain type of young will be 12½% or more they are preceded by ↑ and where the percentage is believed to be less than 12½% the colour will be preceded by ↓

Fawn Cock x Light Back Hen
→ 50% Normal/Fawn & Light Back Cocks, 50% Fawn Hens

Light Back Cock x Fawn Hen
→ 50% Normal/Fawn & Light Back Cocks, 50% Light Back Hens

187

Normal/Fawn & Light Back Cock x Fawn Hen	→	↑ Normal/Fawn & Light Back Cocks, ↑ Fawn Cocks, ↓ Normal/Fawn Cocks, ↓ Fawn/Light Back Cocks, ↑ Fawn Hens, ↑ Light Back Hens, ↓ Normal Hens, ↓ Fawn Light Back Hens
Normal/Fawn & Light Back Cock x Light Back Hen	→	↑ Normal/Fawn & Light Back Cocks, ↑ Light Back Cocks, ↓ Normal/Light Back Cocks, ↓ Light Back/Fawn Cocks, ↑ Light Back Hens, ↑ Fawn Hens, ↓ Normal Hens, ↓ Fawn Light Back Hens
Normal/Fawn & Light Back Cock x Fawn Light Back Hen	→	↑ Fawn/Light Back Cocks, ↑ Light Back/Fawn Cocks, ↓ Normal/Fawn & Light Back Cocks, ↓ Fawn Light Back Cocks, ↑ Fawn Hens, ↑ Light Back Hens, ↓ Normal Hens, ↓ Fawn Light Back Hens
Light Back Cock x Fawn Light Back Hen	→	50% Light Back/Fawn Cocks, 50% Light Back Hens
Fawn Cock x Fawn Light Back Hen	→	50% Fawn/Light Back Cocks, 50% Fawn Hens
Fawn/Light Back Cock x Light Back Hen	→	25% Normal/Fawn & Light Back Cocks, 25% Light Back/Fawn Cocks, 25% Fawn Hens, 25% Fawn Light Back Hens
Fawn/Light Back Cock x Fawn Hen	→	25% Fawn Cocks, 25% Fawn/Light Back Cocks, 25% Fawn Hens, 25% Fawn Light Back Hens
Light Back/Fawn Cock x Light Back Hen	→	25% Light Back Cocks, 25% Light Back/Fawn Cocks, 25% Light Back Hens, 25% Fawn Light Back Hens
Light Back/Fawn Cock x Fawn Hen	→	25% Normal/Fawn & Light Back Cocks, 25% Fawn/Light Back Cocks, 25% Light Back Hens, 25% Fawn Light Back Hens
Fawn/Light Back Cock x Fawn Light Back Hen	→	25% Fawn/Light Back Cocks, 25% Fawn Light Back Cocks, 25% Fawn Hens, 25% Fawn Light Back Hens
Light Back/Fawn Cock x Fawn Light Back Hen	→	25% Light Back/Fawn Cocks, 25% Fawn Light Back Cocks, 25% Light Back Hens, 25% Fawn Light Back Hens

Fawn Light Back Cock x Fawn Hen	→	50% Fawn/Light Back Cocks, 50% Fawn Light Back Hens
Fawn Light Back Cock x Light Back Hen	→	50% Light Back/Fawn Cocks, 50% Fawn Light Back Hens
Fawn Light Back Cock x Fawn Light Back Hen	→	100% Fawn Light Back Cocks and Hens

It is possible for two slightly different types of Normal/Fawn and Light Back Cocks to exist. One has the two mutant genes for Fawn and Light Back on different X chromosomes, and the other carries the two mutant genes on the same X chromosome. This difference can marginally alter the percentages of young produced from matings which include Normal/Fawn and Light Back Cocks.

Although Chestnut Flanked White, being a sex-linked mutation, can be substituted for Light Back in the above matings, it cannot be substituted for Fawn. The C.F.W. and Light Back mutant genes occur in the same position on the X chromosome and therefore matings between the two colours produce unique results.

Chestnut Flanked White x *Light Back*

C.F.W. Cock x Light Back Hen	→	50% Light Back/C.F.W. Cocks, 50% C.F.W. Hens
Light Back Cock x C.F.W. Hen	→	50% Light Back/C.F.W. Cocks, 50% Light Back Hens
Light Back/C.F.W. Cock x Light Back Hen	→	25% Light Back Cocks, 25% Light Back/C.F.W. Cocks, 25% Light Back Hens, 25% C.F.W. Hens
Light Back/C.F.W. Cock x C.F.W. Hen	→	25% Light Back/C.F.W. Cocks, 25% C.F.W. Cocks, 25% Light Back Hens, 25% C.F.W. Hens
Light Back/C.F.W. Cock x Normal Hen	→	25% Normal/Light Back Cocks, 25% Normal/C.F.W. Cocks, 25% Light Back Hens, 25% C.F.W. Hens

Dark Skinned C.F.W. x *Pale Skinned C.F.W.*

Dark C.F.W. Cock x Pale C.F.W. Hen	→	50% Dark C.F.W./Pale C.F.W. Cocks, 50% Dark C.F.W. Hens
Pale C.F.W. Cock x Dark C.F.W. Hen	→	50% Dark C.F.W./Pale C.F.W. Cocks, 50% Pale C.F.W. Hens
Dark C.F.W./Pale C.F.W. Cock x Dark C.F.W. Hen	→	25% Dark C.F.W. Cocks, 25% Dark C.F.W./Pale C.F.W. Cocks, 25% Dark C.F.W. Hens, 25% Pale C.F.W. Hens

Dark C.F.W./Pale C.F.W.   →   25% Dark C.F.W./Pale C.F.W.
  Cock x Pale C.F.W. Hen   Cocks, 25% Pale C.F.W. Cocks,
                                   25% Dark C.F.W. Hens, 25% Pale
                                   C.F.W. Hens

The terms Dark and Pale refer to the skin colour of young chicks and do not relate to the feather colour of Chestnut Flanked Whites. A full explanation of these two different types is provided in the chapter devoted to Chestnut Flanked Whites.

I have attempted to include as many useful matings as possible and further indications as to the pairings most commonly used for each colour are given in the chapters covering the specific colours. Some of the matings given are of little practical use, but they have been included to highlight possible pitfalls. In general terms, pairings which produce young of a known genetic make-up are to be preferred. For example, if a mating produces 25 per cent Normal and 50 per cent Normal/Pied youngsters, the only way to differentiate between the two types is by test mating each Normal produced. Should you wish to breed Normal/Pied youngsters, try to use a mating where all the visual Normals produced are split for Pied.

In pairings intended to breed Dominant Dilutes, it appears that much more productive results are obtained when using double factor birds rather than single factor birds. Unfortunately there are very few double factor birds available, due largely to the practice of seldom pairing two Dominant Dilutes together. Matings which include double factor Dilutes have been included so that a more complete picture, with regard to dominant inheritance, can be ascertained.

It may be of interest to know that the Zebra Finch Society has published a very useful booklet, compiled by M.S. Wrenn and I.E. Whiston, which details nearly 250 different matings. For those interested in the colour expectations of different mutations of Zebra Finch, it is a very worthwhile acquisition.

Bibliography

Pizzey, G., *Field Guide to Birds of Australia*, Collins

Stamp, D. *The World*, Longman Group

Whiston, I. E. and Wrenn, M. S., *The Zebra Finch Society Matings List and Colour Expectations*, Zebra Finch Society (1977)

The Zebra Finch Society Handbook 1984–6

Index

Entries followed by a † are illustrated in the colour section

4353